Magari Auga

鈎 逢賀

サムライ剣舞シアター 代表

今に生きる ″サムライ″ の美

剣舞入門

Kenbu
A performing art
shaped by
samurai
aesthetics

青幻舎

勇壮な紋付袴姿で、すり足で舞台に出で立ち、勢いよく抜刀。扇を取り出し散り花の見立てをして命の儚さを表す。前方には詩文を朗々と力強く詠ずる吟士……。武士（侍）が興した芸能、剣舞です。

剣舞は「吟剣詩舞」とも呼ばれ、漢詩や和歌に独特の節を付けて詠う詩吟（吟詠）に合わせて、刀や扇で舞う日本の古典的な舞台芸能です。江戸時代末期の若い侍たちが、日本の将来を憂いて刀を持って舞ったことが源流とされ、明治初期～中期にかけて全国的に舞台芸能として広まりました。武士の精神性や文化を現代に遺す芸能といえます。本書は、剣舞をまだよく知らない方のために、剣舞がどのような芸能であるか、その鑑賞法や習い方を解説する、いわば初心者向けの解説本です。

現在、剣舞の流派は国内に一〇〇以上あるといわれ、多くの人が日夜稽古に励み、全国のホールで途切れることなく舞台が行われています。また、高校の文化系部活動のインターハイ「全国高等学校総合文化祭」にも吟詠剣詩舞部門があり、毎年多くの高校生が出場しています。

しかしながら、剣舞に少しでも触れたことのある方なら

Foreword

Valiantly dressed in a crested kimono and hakama, the performer vigorously draws his sword for successive displays of fencing techniques while shuffling across the stage. He uses his fan to imitate fallen petals as an expression of the vanity of life, accompanied by the sonorously energetic voice of a poetry reciter in the foreground.

Such is kenbu, a performing art established by samurai.

Kenbu, also known as *ginkenshibu*, is a Japanese classical performing art that combines dance with a sword or fan, and shigin (or gin'ei) recitals of Chinese or Japanese poems with unique melodies. Kenbu allegedly originated from performances by young people in the late Edo period who, concerned about the future of Japan, took to the stage while wielding their swords. Kenbu eventually became popular as a stage art across Japan in the late 19th century, and can be understood as a performing art that has been conserving the samurai spirit and culture up to the present age. For people unfamiliar with kenbu, this book is a "beginner's guide" so to speak that outlines the characteristics of kenbu as a performing art, while also offering tips and suggestions regarding its practice and appreciation.

お気づきかと思いますが、世の中では剣舞の知名度はまだまだ高くありません。「剣舞を習っている」と言って「剣舞って何？」と聞かれる体験をしたことがある人はほぼ一〇〇％でしょう。また、剣舞に関する書籍を書店で探すことはとても難しく、お師匠さんから技術を習い、ちょっとした歴史を見聞きする以外で、その全体像を知る機会は非常に乏しいといえます。

剣舞が舞台芸能として成立して約一五〇年たちました　が、日本の芸能史全体から見れば一五〇年という長さは「伝統」というよりも、一つの「運動」の段階に過ぎないという見方ができます。剣舞について、今できる限りの説明をして、整理していくことは、今後剣舞が更に発展していくために、必要不可欠なことだと考えています。本書で、筆者が日頃剣舞について考えていることをご紹介することで、より多くの方に剣舞に興味を持っていただきたい。また、剣舞に関わる方々の知識補完としてお役立ていただきたい。そして、皆で意見を交わす材料にしていただくことで、一〇〇年先の剣舞がもっと活発な状況になっていれば……、と願っています。

ここで、筆者について簡単に自己紹介しましょう。

It is said that there exist today more than one hundred kenbu schools in Japan where countless pupils exercise day and night, and kenbu performances are being staged in venues all over the country. Many high school students participate in the gin'ei kenchibu sections at annual interscholastic meetings of culture-related high school clubs. However, as everyone who knows a little bit about kenbu has probably noticed, the recognition of kenbu among the genral public is still rather low. More or less everyone who practices kenbu probably shares the experience of telling people about kenbu and being asked what that is. Searches for anything on kenbu in bookstores tend to be largely fruitless, and other than learning techniques from a kenbu master or gathering some historical facts, there are very few occasions for grasping the whole picture.

About 150 years have passed since kenbu was first established as a form of performing arts, and within the context of Japanese performing art history at large, it would be fair to say that a period of just 150 years indicates a "fashion" rather than a "tradition." Regarding the future of kenbu, I believe that it is essential to illustrate and arrange things as much as possible today, and thereby create a foundation for kenbu to develop further. By sharing in this book the various thoughts related to kenbu that cross my mind every day, I hope to get a much larger number of people interested in kenbu, while also hoping that the book will provide everyone involved with kenbu with some extra knowledge. Finally, it is my desire to help facilitate dialogue and exchange about kenbu, to ensure that there will be an even livelier kenbu scene in 100

筆者は「正賀流（せいがりゅう）」という関西の小さな剣舞流派の家に生まれました。幼少からお弟子さんに囲まれ、いつも玩具がわりに扇子があり、二歳の時には木刀を振ってお稽古らしきことをしていたという、典型的な宗家一家の環境で育ちました。ところが、素直にお稽古していたのは小学生低学年まで。高学年になると、周りに剣舞を理解してくれる友達がいないことに気づき、学校文化祭の舞台発表で剣舞を披露すれば笑いが起こるなど、子どもながらに剣舞には価値も将来性もないと思うようになっていました。中学から大学まではほとんど稽古にも舞台にも参加せず、将来は海外転勤もあるような企業やNGOで働きたいという夢を描くようになりました。

転機は二〇〇八年。就職が決まってゆとりのある学生生活を過ごしていた時期、たまたま自宅近くにできたカルチャーセンターで講師募集があり、思い出づくりのような気持ちで剣舞講座を始めました。その時、初めて剣舞に触れた三人のお弟子さん（いずれも当時六十代の人生の大先輩）が口々に、「こんな素晴らしい芸能があるなんて、もっと早くに知りたかった……！」と仰ったのです。筆者には当たり前のように身近にあり、にもかかわらず世間の人には認めてもらえないと思っていた剣舞が、その

years from now.

At this occasion, allow me to introduce myself in a few lines.

I was born into a family that has been running a small kenbu school called "Seiga-ryu" in the Kansai region. I grew up surrounded by pupils, playing with fans rather than toys, and when I was two years old, I did my first lessons (or something like that) with a wooden sword. But even though it was a typical environment for the daughter of a school founder to grow up in, I only studied seriously until I was in the lower grades of elementary school. As a high school student I realized that none of my friends were showing any interest in kenbu, and as my kenbu performances at school fetivals earned only laughter, I came to believe that kenbu was something with no value and no future. From junior high school up to university, I rarely attended any lessons or performances, and began to dream of working for a company or NGO where I would possibly be transferred overseas instead.

The turning point came in 2008. Just when I had found employment and sat back to enjoy the rest of my student days, a culture center happened to open in the neighborhood. They were looking for instructors, and I eventually started giving kenbu lessons there, mostly for "memory-making" purposes. Three of my students that had encountered kenbu for the first time (and that were already in their sixties) would often comment that they "wished [they'd] learned about this wonderful performing art much earlier!" I was greatly surprised to see kenbu, which I grew up with quite naturally, but

うに魅力あるものに映ることは驚きでした。そして初めて剣舞の魅力や価値について真剣に考えるようになりました。さらに、「剣舞が世に知られていないのは、これまで知ってもらうための努力をしてこなかったからではないか?」「知ってもらえるようになれば、自分自身も剣舞家としてやりがいや自信を持てるのではないか?」「そのための活動をすることは、剣舞を心底好きとは思えない今の自分だからこそ出来るのではないか?」と思い至ったのです。

そして二〇一〇年、流派活動の一環として「サムライ剣舞体験ツアー」を立ち上げました。剣舞の教室に入門していない観光客や外国人の方が、気軽に剣舞を体験できるミニツアーです。ここで、お客さんの率直な感想を聞き、苦労しながら説明をしていくうちに、自分の中で剣舞に対して様々な見方ができるようになりました。現在は、会社として流派から独立、京都と東京の二か所で、常設の剣舞体験・演舞場「サムライ剣舞シアター」を運営しています。海外の方を含め年間五千人以上のお客様が訪れてくださるようになりましたが、皆さんいずれも、剣舞師(色々な流派の若手師範ら)の迫力ある舞や体験指導を通して、剣舞の魅力を存分に感じてくださり、「もっと剣

that people in general seemed rather indifferent about, being received with such enthusiasm. It was an experience that inspired me to think for the first time rather seriously about the appeal and value of kenbu, which resulted in such conclusions as "The fact that kenbu is largely unknown is perhaps mainly due to a lack of effort to make it known;" "If more people knew about kenbu, that might boost also my own confidence and sense of fulfillment as a kenbu performer;" and "I may be able to dedicate myself to such activities just because I don't seem to love kenbu 'from the bottom of my heart' at this point."

In 2010, as part of our school's activities, I launched the "Samurai Kenbu Experience Tour" a mini tour for unexperienced tourists and foreigners to casually get in touch with kenbu. We are doing our best to explain things to participants while asking them to give us their frank opinions, and in that process, I have developed an ability to apply a variety of different viewpoints on kenbu myself. At present, the company is independent from the school, and operates "Samurai Kenbu Theater" stages for the experience and performance of kenbu at two locations in Kyoto and Tokyo. We have more than 5,000 visitors including foreign tourists every year, who get to sense the fascination of kenbu through their experiences in trial lessons or overwhelming performances by kenbu masters (young instructors from various schools), and frequently get in touch because they "want to know more" or "look for places to practice kenbu after returning home from Japan." I am really happy about that.

舞について知りたい」「旅行から帰った後も地元で習えるところはないか」と、問合せをしてくださいます。本当に嬉しい限りです。

そんな経緯で、本来であれば、三十代の筆者が、業界の大先輩らを差し置いて剣舞のイロハを語って本を出すなんてことは、多分におこがましいことと承知しているのですが、シアターの滞在時間だけでは伝えきれない剣舞の知識や魅力を伝えるには、本を読んでもらうのが手っ取り早いと思い、出版をお願いすることになりました。また、外国の方にも伝えたいという思いから、本書はバイリンガル仕様になっています。昨今のインバウンドブームも手伝って、世界中で侍や日本文化への注目が高まる中、武士の文化や精神性を遺す剣舞が持つ可能性は非常に大きいと感じています。本書が国境を越えて様々な読者の手に届けば幸いです。

本書は三章で構成されています。

「第一章 剣舞を知る・観る」では、剣舞を「観る側」として楽しむための基本知識やエッセンスを紹介します。

「第二章 剣舞を習う・舞う」では、剣舞を習う・演じる側として知っておきたいこと。流派への入門の仕方、お

Considering these circumstances, putting out a book and talking about the 101 of kenbu over the heads of all the veterans in the business would normally be an impertinent thing to do for a woman in her thirties like myself, but I thought that a book was the quickest way to communicate all the knowledge and the appeal of kenbu that is difficult to get across during people's short stays at the theaters. As I want to reach also people outside Japan, when making the decision to put the book together, it was clear for me that it was going to be completely bilingual. With increasing numbers of foreign tourists visiting Japan in recent years, and a growing worldwide interest in samurai and various other aspects of Japanese culture, I feel that kenbu has a lot of potential as a performing art that conserves the samurai culture and spirit. I hope that this book will find its way across national borders, and into the hands of a variety of readers around the world.

The book is divided into three chapters.

Chapter 1, titled "Knowledge and Appreciation of Sword Dance," introduces essential facts and basic knowledge for a rather profound enjoyment of kenbu from the spectator's side.

Chapter 2 "Training and Performance of Sword Dance" focuses on things that are helpful to know for everyone who practices and/or performs kenbu. In this chapter I explain kenbu school enrollment methods, manners and basic techniques.

Chapter 3 "Deeper and Wider" addresses the history and artistic qualities of kenbu, and features interviews with the heads

作法、基本的な技術解説などを行います。

「第三章　剣舞を深める・広げる」では、剣舞の歴史や、芸道論、全国の先生方へのインタビューなど、剣舞をもっと楽しむ為に幅広く考察する広場の位置づけにしました。歴史と芸道論については、筆者が3年前に2回目の大学となる京都造形芸術大学通信教育部にて提出したエッセイ（卒業論文）を、本書用に編集したものです。少し専門的な内容も含まれますが、剣舞を習っている方や、指導をしている方にもぜひ読んでいただきたい章です。

最後に、本書の制作・出版にあたり、株式会社青幻舎の山本大揮様、久下まり子様、編集の谷脇栗太様、HON DESIGNの北尾崇様、翻訳のアンドレアス・シュトゥールマン様、その他にも多くの方に多大なご協力をいただきました。この場を借りて、心より御礼を申し上げます。

of schools across Japan. This chapter is designed as a platform for discussion and food for thought, with the aim to enhance the reader's fun with kenbu. It contains outlines of historical and artistic contexts that have been rewritten based on a graduation thesis that I originally submitted to the Correspondence Education department of the Kyoto University of Art and Design three years ago. There are some rather technical parts, but it's a chapter that is surely worth reading also for everyone who practices or teaches kenbu.

Finally, I would like to take this opportunity to express my heartfelt thanks to Yamamoto Hiroki, Kuge Mariko and editor Taniwaki Kurita from Seigensha Art Publishng Inc., as well as Kitao Takashi from HON DESIGN, translator Andreas Stuhlmann, and everyone else involved, for their cooperation in the making and publication of this book.

A 1-page guide to "kenbu" and the "samurai" culture it emerged from

Kenbu is a form of performing arts created by samurai. While there have existed a variety of warrior groups around the world, the "samurai" were a rather exceptional case of a group that has become widely known under a specific proper name. The following overview of the history and relationship between kenbu and samurai illustrates what kind of people the samurai were, and what prompted them to start performing kenbu.

Originating from the verb "saburau," the term "samurai" was initially used to refer to men who served and guarded aristocrats in the Heian period. These are considered to be the predecessors of the samurai as they later became famous. In the 12th century, Minamoto no Yoritomo established the Kamakura shogunate, marking the beginning of a samurai government that would last for seven centuries. As entrusting one's life to someone else was not an uncommon idea in the samurai society, the focus was not only on the refinement of military arts, but also the building of trusting relationships was regarded as important. During the time of the Muromachi shogunate in the 14th century, there were public meeting spaces called "kaijo" in Kyoto, and those were places where various cultural activities such as the tea ceremony, ikebana or renga poetry developed.

During the Sengoku era in the 16th century, the samurai's aim to become the rulers of Japan sparked a string of fierce battles in all parts of the country. Some of the military commanders at the time went down in history. In order to exhibit their power and confidence, they were also very particular about their armor and helmets, and their displays of braveness became the foundation the kata (patterns) in kenbu are based on. In the early 17th century, the Tokugawa clan established a shogunate in Edo (Tokyo), and thereby brought peace to the country that eventually prevailed for about 250 years. From there, the samurai developed a unique set of values and mentality that is still being referred to as "bushido" today. This philosophy is summed up by such attitudes as "being loyal to the lord," "valuing courtesy," "bravely executing what is correct," and "treating the weak with affection."

In 1853, the American "Perry squadron" arrived in Japan. Not only the shogunate, but also the local samurai sensed in this situation a threat to the autonomy of Japan, and engaged in heated discussions about the future of their country. Some of them chose to express their thoughts and feelings through Chinese-style poems, which they recited while dancing with their swords and fans. The additional element of poetry recitation (shigin) in kenbu allowed performers to express next to the braveness of the samurai also much more subtle emotional aspects. Through such activities, the local samurai finally managed to overthrow the shogunate.

In 1867, the announcement of the return of political power from the Edo shogunate to the emperor at Nijo Castle in Kyoto (which is today a word heritage site) marked the end of the age of samurai. While various forms of Western culture were aggressively imported, in the newly implemented class system it was forbidden to wear a sword, which forced many fencing dojo (training studios) to close. Terrified at the prospect of the samurai culture their forefathers had forged getting lost altogether, the master swordsmen began to stage fencing performances that hadn't been shown in public up to that point. That was also when the first kenbu performances were carried out. Such performances gained popularity, and quickly spread across the whole country. In 1890, Hibino Raifu established a school specializing in kenbu in Tokyo, after which a variety of schools opened one after another that still exist today. This was the beginning of kenbu as a traditional performing art.

"サムライ"の伝統から生まれた "剣舞"とは

剣舞は侍が興した舞台芸能です。世界には様々な戦闘集団がありますが、「侍」のように固有名詞で知られている例はそれほど多くありません。侍がどのような人々なのか、なぜ彼らが剣舞を興したのか、それぞれの歴史と関係性をざっくりと説明します。

侍は「さぶらふ」を語源とし、もともとは平安時代に貴族に仕え警護をしていた人たちのことを指します。

十二世紀、源頼朝が鎌倉幕府を開き、以後七〇〇年に及ぶ、侍が国を治める時代が始まりました。侍の社会では、他人に命を預けることもあることから、武芸を磨くだけでなく、信頼関係の構築が重視されました。そのため、十四世紀の京都の室町幕府では「会所」という公的な寄り合いの場が設けられ、そこで茶や華道、連歌など多くの文化が発達しました。

十六世紀の戦国時代、侍は天下人をめざして各地で激しい戦いを繰り広げます。歴史に名を刻む武将達も登場します。彼らは自信や力強さを見せつけるため、兜や鎧にもこだわりました。このように侍が勇ましさを表現する姿は、剣舞の型の源流ともなっています。十七世紀初頭、徳川家により江戸に幕府が開かれ、およそ二五〇年にわたる平和な世が訪れます。そこから彼

らは、現代では「武士道」とも呼ばれる独特の精神性と価値観を築くことになります。「主君に忠義を尽くす」、「礼節を重んじる」、「正しいことは敢然と実行する」、「弱き者には慈愛をもって接する」などは、その代表的な考え方です。

一八五三年、アメリカの「ペリー艦隊」が日本に来航します。日本の独立が侵されかねない状況に、幕府だけでなく、地方の武士までが日本の未来について激しく議論しました。彼らの一部は自分の考えや気持ちを漢詩として詠み、その詩を吟じながら刀と扇を持って表現しました。漢詩の吟（詩吟）を伴うことにより、剣舞は武士の勇ましさだけでなく、細やかな心情を表現できるようになりました。こうした地方武士の働きは、いよいよ倒幕へと向かいます。

一八六七年、ついに京都の二条城（世界遺産）で、江戸幕府から天皇に政権が返還することが宣言され、武士の世が終わりました。欧米文化が積極的に取り入れられる一方、新しい身分制度の下で帯刀を禁じられ、多くの剣術道場が閉鎖されました。そうした中、剣豪たちは、先祖が築き上げた侍の文化が失われることを危惧し、それまで公に披露されることのなかった剣術試合の興行と、剣舞の公演を始めました。公演は人気を博し、全国に広がっていきます。明治二十三年に東京の日比野雷風が剣舞を専門とする流派を創設し、以後現代まで続く様々な流派が生まれることになりました。

これが、伝統舞台芸能としての剣舞の始まりです。

content

全国の宗家にインタビュー ———

Interviews

第一章

剣舞を
知る
見る

Chapter
I
Knowledge and
Appreciation of
Kenbu

剣舞の
始まり

幕末の志士が
刀を手に舞い始めた

剣舞はいつから始まったのか？　物事の始まりをいつとするかは、どんなことであっても難しいものです。

大陸から日本へ刀剣が伝来した時にはすでに刀で舞うという文化も一緒に伝わったかもしれませんし、刀で舞ったことだけで見れば、太平記（十四世紀の軍記物語）にそのような記載があります。しかしこれらは今の剣舞の歴史に直接繋がるものではなく、源流というには隔たりがあるように

撃剣興行の図（撃剣会之図）
1873（明治6）年、国立国会図書館蔵

思います。

剣舞にとって直接の源流といえば、やはり江戸末期に昌平坂学問所の学生が酒に酔って漢詩を吟じつつ刀を抜いたというのが有名で、一番分かりやすいスタートといえるでしょう。

剣舞家の中には、刀は簡単に抜くものではないという武道的な考えから、この説を嫌う人もいます。ただ、筆者にとってはこのエピソードこそ、剣舞の起源として重要だと思っています。

昌平坂学問所といえば、現在の東京大学です。列強が日本に押し寄せる中、勉学に励む学生が国の行く末を憂いて漢詩を詠み、刀を抜いて気持ちを表現したことは、剣舞を舞う動機（なぜ武士が剣を抜いて舞う必要があったのかの理由）として、とても納得がいくように思いますし、他の芸能にはないオリジナルの価値観ではないかと思います。

The Origins of Kenbu

The leaders of the late Tokugawa period were the first to perform dances with their swords.

As in any other field, the question "when it all began" is difficult to answer precisely also in the case of kenbu. When the sword itself was brought to Japan from the Asian continent, the tradition of using it in dance performances may have been imported at the same time. In terms of records of "dancing with a sword," such practices have been mentioned as early as in the "Taiheiki" (a war chronicle of the 14th century). But there is no historical connection between those practices and today's kenbu, and it seems that there is a gap regarding the respective origins.

About the direct origins of kenbu, there exists a popular theory that drunken students of the Shoheizaka school were the first to draw their swords while chanting classical Chinese poems, and this may be the easiest explanation of how the tradition of sword dance started. Some kenbu practitioners, however, reject this theory, based on the martial artistic idea that the sword is a tool that isn't all that easy to handle. Anyway, personally I consider the aforementioned episode to be rather essential when it comes to defining the origins of kenbu.

The Shoheizaka school was in fact the predecessor of today's University of Tokyo. The idea that, against the backdrop of the surge of the Great Powers, devoted students used Chinese poetry and their swords to express their anxiety about the future of their country, sounds very reasonable as a motive for samurai to draw their swords and dance with them, and this is where I seem to detect an original kind of value that doesn't exist in other forms of performing arts.

撃剣興行が
舞台芸能としてのスタート

剣舞の舞台芸能としての起源は、明治六年に、剣術家・榊原鍵吉が、剣術道場衰退への対策として始めた撃剣興行です。これは、相撲興行に倣って剣術の試合を大衆に見せるものですが、試合の合間の余興として剣舞を行ったことで、一躍世に知られることになりました。撃剣興行、そして剣舞は全国でまたたく間に場を増やし、人気を博しました。そのうちに、撃剣家の一人、日比野雷風が東京で神刀流を創流し、吟士に合わせて剣士が舞う現在の剣舞のスタイルを確立しました。神刀流の他にもいくつかの元となる流派があり、それらからの分派を経て、いわゆるお稽古ごととしての剣舞が世に定着しました。

日比野雷風　神刀流提供

Hibino Raifu

榊原鍵吉　国立国会図書館蔵

Sakakibara Kenkichi

The beginning of show fencing as a form of performing arts

The origins of kenbu as a performing art go back to 1873, when the swordsman Sakakibara Kenkichi began to show *kenjutsu* (swordplay) performances, called *Gekiken* fencing show, as a measure against the decline of *kenjutsu dojo* (training halls). In the manner of sumo wrestling, kenjutsu matches used to be staged in front of the general public, with sword dance performances inserted for entertainment between the matches. This is how kenbu became widely known at one bound, and *Gekiken* fencing show and kenbu rapidly increased and gained popularity all across Japan. One of the kenjutsu masters at the time was Hibino Raifu, who founded the Shinto-ryu (Shinto school) in Tokyo, and thereby established the style of present-day kenbu combining poetry recitation and dance with swords and fans. Next to the Shinto-ryu, there exist a number of other schools as well that helped originate kenbu, and it is via branches of such schools that kenbu established itself as something to be practiced in *okeikogoto* ("individual enrichment courses").

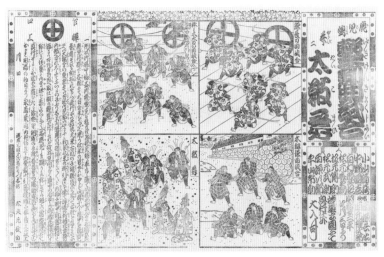

見世物興行の番組表（鹿児島撃剣曲試合 太皷舞） 早稲田大学演劇博物館蔵
"Kagoshima Gekiken with music and dance" show program

剣舞の
あれこれ

読み方によって
違う芸能に？

剣舞は、文字通りの意味としては、剣の舞（Sword dance）、あるいは剣を使って舞うこと全体を指しますが、日本の古典芸能の枠組みに限った場合、「剣舞」という表記をする芸能には次の大きく三つがあります。

剣舞
神楽の中で舞われる剣の舞。

剣舞
岩手県の郷土芸能。「鬼剣舞」「念仏剣舞」とも。

剣舞
吟詠（詩吟）に合わせて舞う、武士由来の芸能。「吟剣詩舞」とも。

本書で取り上げているのは、三つ目の「けんぶ」です。同じ漢字、同じ剣を使う舞であっても、様式や目的、舞手に至るまで、全く別物の芸能が三つも存在することに、驚かれ

るかもしれません。この他にも、例えば時代劇などで活躍する殺陣師が刀剣を持って舞に近い演出をする時に、「剣舞」と称することがあります。時代劇俳優＝武士の姿なので、右の分類では「けんぶ」が一番近く、観る側にとっても「剣舞」という表現がとても自然に聞こえるのですが、それは単に「剣を使った舞」を「剣舞」（広義の剣舞）と称しているのであり、日本の古典的な芸能の一ジャンルとしての「剣舞」ではありません。

神楽の一種「剣舞（けんまい）」
宇城市教育委員会提供

Kenmai: A form of sword dance as part of a ritual Kagura performance at a Shinto festival

岩手県北上市北上みちのく芸能
まつり鬼剣舞（けんばい）

Kenbai: A local form of performing arts in Iwate Prefecture

Things to know about kenbu

Different art forms depending on the pronunciation?

The term "剣舞 (kenbu) " consists of the Chinese characters 剣 (sword) and 舞 (dance), so the literal meaning would be "sword dance," or generally a "dance involving swords." Within the framework of Japanese classical performing arts, there are three main art forms that are written "剣舞" but pronounced differently.

Kenmai: A form of sword dance as part of a ritual *Kagura* performance at a Shinto festival.
Kenbai: A local form of performing arts in Iwate Prefecture. Also known as *Onikenbai* (devil's sword dance) or Nenbutsu *kenbai* (Buddhist invocation sword dance).
Kenbu: A form of dance that is derived from samurai culture, and performed along with poetry recitation (ginei, or shigin). Also known as Ginkenshibu.

The one we talk about in this book is kenbu. It may sound odd that there exist three completely different kinds of performing arts in terms of style, purpose and performers even though their names all consists of the same characters for "sword" and "dance." In ad-dition, we also speak of "kenbu" when sword fight arrangers ap-pearing in historical plays, for example, make dancelike moves with their swords. As we talk about actors appearing as samurai in historical plays, kenbu seems to be the appropriate name according to the above classification, and for the viewer, "剣舞" may be the most natural term to describe it. However this is simply a "dance using swords" that is referred to as "剣舞" ("sword dance" in a broad sense), and it is not kenbu as one genre of Japanese classical performing arts.

業界の人が使う「吟剣詩舞」とは

剣舞の教室を調べたり入門して稽古をしたりしていくと、かならず「吟剣詩舞」という言葉を聞くことになるでしょう。実は、「吟剣詩舞」を辞書や事典で調べても該当しません。

これは、吟剣詩舞が、吟詠（または詩吟）・剣舞・詩舞（または扇舞）の三つの総称であり、それ自体を一つの芸能として発表した学術資料がないからです。

吟詠（詩吟）とは、東西古今の漢詩、和歌、俳句などに独特の節をつけて吟ずることをいいます。

そして、詩舞とは、剣舞から派生した扇のみで舞うものをいいます。詩舞は扇舞とも呼ばれ、もとは、女性が刀を持つのは相応しくないとの考えから、刀を扇に持ち替えて舞っ

たことが始まりです。吟詠は、声楽ジャンルの一つであるため、それだけでも成立する独立性の高い技芸といえます。一方、剣舞・詩舞は、その詩吟に合わせて舞うことで、詩の内容を表現するものですから、基本的には詩吟が必要不可欠となります。

そのため、吟詠・剣舞・詩舞は一体となって活動することが多く、三つを合わせて「吟剣詩舞」（または「吟詠剣詩舞」、「吟舞」とも）と業界では呼んでいるのです。

本書でも、詩舞も含めて語るときは「剣詩舞」、吟詠も含めてお話をするときは「吟剣詩舞」と表記することがあります。

Professional Ginkenshibu

When doing research about kenbu training, or entering a school as a pupil, at some point one inevitably comes across the expression *ginkenshibu*. As a matter of fact, the term is not included in any Japanese dictionary, because *ginkenshibu* is a collective term that incorporates *ginei* (or *shigin*), kenbu and *shibu* (or *senbu*; fan dance), and there exist no academic documents in which it is stated as a form of performing arts in its own right.

The term *ginei* (*shigin*) has been universally used to refer to the recitation of classical Chinese, tanka or haiku poetry with additional original melodies.

Derived from kenbu, *shibu* is the name of a dance that is performed with a fan only. It is also known as *senbu*, and originates from the practice of women dancing with a fan instead of a sword, based on the idea that it is inappropriate for a woman to carry a sword. As *ginei* is a genre of vocal music, it can be considered as an independent art form in and by itself, whereas kenbu and *shibu* are performed to accompany poems and communicate their contents, so for them the poetry recital is generally an essential part. This is how *ginei*, kenbu and *shibu* came to be performed together as a set that is commonly referred to as *ginkenshibu* (also *ginei-kenshibu* or *ginbu*).

In this book, sword dance is referred to as *kenshibu* when it is discussed as an art form that contains *shibu* elements, and as *ginkenshibu* as a form that involves *ginei* recitation.

愛好者はどれくらい？

昔に比べると流派の数はどんどん減っていますが、それでも全国に百以上の流派があるといわれています。

しかし、流派に所属し稽古をする門下生の数は、流派により一名～五百名超と多様で、通常非公開のため、おおよその人数を示すことも困難です。一説には五千～一万人といわれることがありますが、業界の実感に近いと思います。一部の流派は海外にも支部があり、外国人の愛好者もいます。剣舞の流派を取りまとめる団体としては、公益財団法人日本吟剣詩舞振興会と全日本剣詩舞道連盟の二つが知られています。流派ごとに行われる発表会やリサイタルのほかに、これら団体が主催する大規模な大会が年に数度行われています。

また、学校教育においては、高校の部活動に「吟詠剣詩舞道部」を擁するところがあり、その多くが毎年の全国高等学校総合文化祭に出場しています。

Following

Even though the number of kenbu schools has decreased dramatically, it is said that there still exist more than one hundred schools across Japan today. The number of pupils studying at each of these schools varies greatly, from one to over five hundred, but as such information is normally undisclosed, it is difficult even to state rough numbers. According to estimates, the total number of pupils is somewhere between five and ten thousand, and based on my own experience in the business, I would confirm this. Some schools maintain branches also outside Japan, so there are also foreigners among the following of kenbu. As collective kenbu school organizations, the Nippon Ginkenshibu Foundation and the All Japan Kenshibudo Federation are well known in Japan. In addition to hosting performances and recitals by each school, these institutions also organize several larger annual events. On the level of school education, there are several high schools that offer "gineikenshibu clubs" for their students' extracurricular activities, many of which regularly partake in the annual nationwide high school culture festival.

他の芸道との比較

剣舞に初めて触れた人からはよく、剣舞は武道なのか、舞なのか、演劇なのかと問われます。武道を経験した人からは、剣道や居合との違いを尋ねられますし、武道よりも舞に馴染みがある人は、日本舞踊や能楽との比較から剣舞について理解しようとします。そして、多くの方にとって、演劇の一種である殺陣との区別がつかないようです。

以下、剣道および居合、日本舞踊、殺陣との違いを簡単に紹介しましょう。

① 剣道・居合

剣道は武道あるいはスポーツで、竹刀を用いて一対一でルールにもとづいて試合を行い、勝敗を決するものです。それに対し、剣舞は、刀と扇を使用し、漢詩などの詩歌に詠まれた内容を舞台上で表現するもので、明確なルールにもとづいて勝敗を決する性格のものではありません。

次に居合は、仮想敵を設定し、敵の動きに対して抜刀し、一撃で相手を制することに主眼を置く武道の一つです。剣舞で用いられる刀法は、居合の抜刀術が基本であり、大いに共通点があります。しかし大きな違いは、漢詩や和歌に合わせるという点と、見た目の美しさを重視するという点です。舞台芸能である剣舞は、個人の技術や内面の精神性が重視されるだけでなく、鑑賞する人の存在を意識し、「美」を追求する発想が中心にあること、そして演出が行われる点が、大きく異なります。

居合
Iaido

©Bobby Coutu

剣道
Kendo

日本舞踊は、広義には日本の踊りの総称であり、剣舞もその一つに数えられますが、狭義には元禄期に歌舞伎から舞踊の要素を抽出して創られた歌舞伎舞踊を指します。歌舞伎舞踊は、元禄期の経済力豊かな町民によって支えられ、形成されてきた

日本舞踊　長唄「扇の寺」吾妻徳穂（東国の白拍子）
花柳寿楽（笛吹く男）

Nihon Buyo

Comparison with other performing and martial arts

People who witness a kenbu performance for the first time often ask whether it is in fact a form of martial arts, dance, or theater. Those with experience in martial arts inquire about how it is different from *kendo* or *iaido*, while those that are more familiar with dance tend to try and understand kenbu by comparing it to classical Japanese dance (*Nihon buyo*) or *Noh*. Generally speaking, for most people it is difficult to grasp the difference between kenbu and "dramatic sword fighting" (*tate*), and without seeing an actual performance.

Below is a simple outline of the differences between *kendo* and *iaido*, Japanese dance, and *tate*.

1) Kendo and Iaido

Kendo is a form of martial arts or sports. Matches are carried out one on one with a bamboo sword, and winners are determined based on rules. Quite differently, in kenbu the contents of Chinese or other forms of poetry are expressed using a sword and/or fan. There don't exist clear rules, and there is no such thing as victory or defeat.

Iaido is a form of marital arts in which the performer draws his or her sword in response to the behavior of an imaginary enemy, with the main purpose of beating the enemy at one stroke. The art of unsheathing the sword as practiced in *iaido* serves at once as a foundation for the basic techniques of kenbu, and there are several characteristics both forms have in common. The main difference however is that kenbu is performed alongside recitals of Chinese or Japanese poetry, with an emphasis on the beautiful visual aspect of the performance. Kenbu as a performing art not only emphasizes individual skills and spiritual inner values, but it is based on the pursuit of "beauty" as a central idea, for which the presence of the audience is always kept in mind. The fact that it is choreographed is another aspect that clearly distinguishes kenbu from the realm of martial arts.

2) Classical Japanese Dance (Nihon Buyo)

Nihon buyo is a collective term that refers to Japanese-style dance in a broad sense, incorporating also kenbu. In a narrow sense, however, it refers to *Kabuki* dance that was established as a dance form in its own right in the Genroku era, based on dance elements borrowed from *Kabuki*. *Kabuki* dance is a form of performing arts that was supported and shaped by economically powerful towns-people in the Genroku era, while kenbu has its origins in kenjutsu, and was developed by samurai who like to practice martial arts. The different forms were established in very different processes, however on can say that various elements, including especially postures and the use of a fan, were largely inspired by Niho buyo.

芸能です。それに対して、剣術を発端とし、武道を嗜む武士らによって作られてきた芸能で、成立過程が大きく異なります。ただ、扇の扱いや所作の面など、日本舞踊から多くを学んでいるといえます。

③ 殺陣（たて）

殺陣は時代劇の映画や舞台における一場面として考案された演劇技術の一種です。刀は軽い竹製やジュラルミンのものが多く、演出監督の指揮のもとで、武道的な確かさよりも立ち回りの激しさや戦いの臨場感といった演出効果が重視されます。それに対し、剣舞は、すり足を基調とした振付により演舞を行い、居合刀など、やや重みのある刀を用い、居合道と共通する稽古も行います。また、多くは家元制度により技が継承される特徴があります。

殺陣
Tate

3) Sword Fighting (Tate)

Tate is a type of staged action that was originally devised for fighting scenes in period dramas and movies. Swords are mostly made of light bamboo, and performances staged after the director's instructions emphasize the dramatic effects of intense hassle and realistic fighting, rather than martial artistic precision. In contrast, kenbu is a choreographed dance that is basically performed in shuffle steps and with rather heavy gear such as practice swords used in iaido. The training is partially identical with iaido training as well. One prominent characteristic is the tradition of mainly handing down techniques through the iemoto (patriarch) system.

舞台の基本構成

最も古典的な吟剣詩舞の舞台は、吟士の声と、刀、扇だけで構成されるシンプルな舞台芸能です。すなわち、舞台の脇に吟士（吟詠を吟じる人）が立ち、舞台中央に舞士（剣舞または詩舞の舞手）が登場します。舞士が「ハッ」などと掛け声を発すると、吟士が吟じ始め、それに合わせて刀や扇で舞います。観客は、吟士の朗々とした吟声に耳を傾け、その詩文の響きを味わうと同時に、舞士の凛々しい舞によって詩文に託されたドラマを楽しみます。大道具や小道具はほとんど必要とせず、初めてその舞台を鑑賞した人は、吟、舞それぞれの迫力にただただ圧倒されることでしょう。

詩吟には、五言絶句や七言絶句など比較的短い漢詩が使われることが多く、他に和歌や俳句もあります。一つの演目の所要時間は三分から五分ほどです。

吟剣詩舞に和楽器の伴奏を取り入れた舞台

Ginkenshibu with musical accompaniment on Japanese instruments

Basic composition

The most basic and classical style of *ginkenshibu* is a simple performance combining only the *ginshi's* voice, a sword and a fan. The *ginshi* (who chants the ginei) stands at the side of the stage, while the *maishi* (the dancer who performs the kenbu or shibu) appears in the center. When the *maishi* shouts something like "Hah!" this is the signal for the *ginshi* to start singing, to which the *maishi* then dances with his or her sword and fan. While listening to the *ginshi's* sonorous recitation and relishing the sound of the recited poem, the audience enjoys at once the *maishi's* manly dance in a dramatic rendition of poetry. Stage sets and props are mostly unnecessary, and those who witness a performance for the first time will probably be overwhelmed by the intense power of the recitation and dance respectively.

For the poetry recitation, comparatively short Chinese poems such as *gogonzekku* or *shichigonzekku* (quatrain with five- or sevencharacter lines) are used most frequently, but there are also waka or haiku poems. The duration of one program is about three to five minutes.

和楽器を使った伴奏が現在の主流

吟に箏や尺八といった日本の伝統楽器の伴奏をつけることも多く、現在はこれが主流となっています。その場合は、「前奏→吟→後奏」という流れになるため、舞士も前奏に合わせて登場します。楽器には銅鑼や鈴などがアクセントとして取り入れられることもあります。戦後は音楽再生機器の発達により、オーケストラの伴奏曲もたくさん販売されています。

照明効果を駆使した演出もある

作品や舞台によっては、複数の舞手による群舞も行われ、よりストーリーが明確に示されるような構成にすることもあります。大きな舞台やリサイタルになると、照明や大道具にも工夫が凝らされます。近年ではシンセサイザーを使用したり、他ジャンルの芸能者とコラボレーションをしたりと、他の伝統舞台芸能と同様に、先進的な取り組みも多数行われています。

Musical accompaniment on Japanese instruments constitute the mainstream today

The singing is often accompanied by performances on such Japanese traditional instruments as *koto* (sou) or *shakuhachi*, and today this style has become mainstream. As the order in this case is overture song postlude, the maishi's appearance is timed with the overture. Next to the koto or the shakuhachi, featured instruments include also the *dora* (gong), bells, and other items to accentuate the musical accompaniment. After the war, the development of musical playback devices resulted in countless orchestra recordings of such accompaniment music.

Arrangements incorporating lighting effects

Depending on the program and the stage, performances may feature group dancing by multiple maishi, or other configurations devised to communicate the story with more clarity. Some large-scale performances and recitals incorporate special lighting or stage sets, and in recent years, synthesizers have come into use as musical instruments. Like in other forms of traditional performing arts, there are various and increasing numbers of forward-looking endeavors, including collaborations with performers from other genres.

舞台を楽しむための3つのポイント

剣舞の有名な作品を一つ挙げると、「不識庵機山を撃つの図に題す」があります。

鞭声粛粛 夜河を過る
暁に見る千兵の大牙を擁するを
遺恨十年 一剣を磨き
流星光底 長蛇を逸す

これは江戸時代後期の武士で漢詩家の頼山陽が、戦国時代の上杉謙信と武田信玄のライバル関係を、上杉謙信の目線で詠んだ漢詩で、「川中島」の通称でよく知られています。

このように、事前に川中島の合戦に関して情報を仕入れたり、漢詩の意味を調べておけば、舞台で何が行われているか、理解しやすくなります。ここでは、剣舞の舞台をより楽しむためのポイントを紹介しましょう。

Three key points for appreciating kenbu

One of the most famous kenbu programs is "Fushikiankizan wo utsu no zu ni daisu."

This classical Chinese-style poem by Rai Sanyo, a samurai and master of Chinese poetry in the late Edo period, illustrates the rivalry between Uesugi Kenshin and Takeda Shingen in the sengoku era of civil wars, from Uesugi Kenshin's point of view. It is also well-known under the popular name "Kawanakajima." The piece thus provides some advance information on the battles of Kawanakajima, and some preliminary research on the meanings of classical Chinese poems can also help understand what is happening on the stage. Below are some points to keep in mind for an enhanced enjoyment of a kenbu performance.

1 Conduct preliminary research on poetry

Whenever you are invited to a recital, contact the organizer and ask for a program or a list of featured poems. As soon as you know what poems will be featured, you can do some research on the Internet, and you may be able to read the poems beforehand. Pre-liminary knowledge of their authors, contents and historical backgrounds help understand the meaning of the choreography of each performance.

1 詩文を予習

発表会やリサイタルに招待された場合、可能であればプログラムもしくは演題リストを主催者にもらえないか、問い合わせてみましょう。演題がわかれば、それをインターネットなどで調べると、詩文を事前に見ることができるかもしれません。吟詠用の漢詩紹介サイトとしては「公益社団法人 関西吟詩文化協会」のサイトが充実しています。詩の作者や内容、歴史背景を予め知っておくと、舞台を見たときにその振り付けが何を意味しているのか、見当がつきやすくなります。

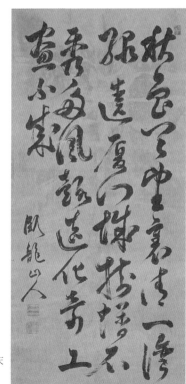

田中綏猷（臥龍山人）自筆秋色天
望雲々　京都大学附属図書館蔵
Tanaka Garyu Sanjin's Poems

2 表現手法を知る

剣舞の振り付けは通常、各流派の宗家・家元・会長、もしくは特別に許しを得た人だけが振りを付けることができます。いくつもの型を組み合わせて（時には新しい型を開発して）、一つの漢詩に振りをつけていきます。

それらの型は大きく以下の三つに分けることができます。表現パターンを沢山知っていれば、目の前で行われている振り付けが何を表しているかを理解することができます。

① 戦いの表現としての刀法

戦う場面では、斬り付けの連続技が用いられます。実際の戦でいつも刀が使われたわけではありませんが、刀を武士の象徴として用います。その際、刀の抜き方や納め方、斬り方など、刀の使術に関する考え方の多くは、居合術がベースになっています。これは、剣舞が武道を元に発展した芸能であるためです。ただ、舞台芸能としての見栄えを重視し、同じ名前がついている型であっても、その所作のあり方が武道と異なることもあります。武道に慣れた方であれば、その違いを発見するのも面白みといえるでしょう。

---

2 Gain knowledge of means of expression

The choreography of a kenbu performance is usually limited to the originator, patriarch or head of the respective school, or other person with special permission. The choreography of a certain Chinese poem is generally carried out by combining several patterns (while sometimes inventing new ones). Patterns can be roughly divided into the three categories described below. The more patterns for expressing certain things you know, the better you will understand the choreography of the piece you are watching.

Sword action expressing a fight

Fighting scenes are expressed through continuous sword strokes. Even though swords were not necessarily used in each and every reallife fight, here the sword is used as a symbol for samurai. Many of the rules for the use of the sword, such as sheathing, unsheathing or striking, are based on the techniques of iaido, which hints at the fact that kenbu is a performing art that developed out of martial arts. Nonetheless, it does stress the showiness of performing arts, and even through some patterns have the same names, the postures in kenbu are sometimes quite different from those in martial arts. For those proficient in martial arts, it may be interesting to try and spot the differences.

②人物の内面描写や、刀や扇の礼法所作

刀を使った振り付けは、斬る型だけではなく、例えば戦の前に刀の手入れをしたり、刀を前に掲げて気持ちの高まりを表すなどの表現もあります。また、座って刀を自分の右脇に、扇を自分の前に置き、主君に対してお辞儀をするなど、実際の扇や刀の礼法所作を振り付けとして見せます。

Psychological descriptions of human characters, and manners of using swords and fans

Choreographies incorporating the use of swords don't only focus on stroke patterns, but they also contain such actions as preparing a sword prior to a fight, or raising the sword in front of the body to express a state of elation. There are also scenes in which actual postures with sword and fan are part of the choreography, such as performers placing their sword to their right and their fan in front of them, and bowing to their lord while seated.

③「見立て」による風俗表現

刀や扇を何か他の事物として表すことを「見立て」といいます。刀であれば、杖、弓、銃など、扇であれば、草木、雨風、山、波、酒、扉、兜、鎧、血しぶき、弓、杖など、情景や心情を幅広く表現することができます。たまに扇に代わって実物の旗や盃、杖に持ち替えたりもしますが、基本的には全て扇や刀で置き換えることが可能です。

Expressions of manners and customs through "mitate"

The style of using a sword or a fan to resemble something else is known as *mitate*. A sword can be used to resemble a cane, a bow or a gun, while a fan can be used for expressing a wide range of things and feelings, including plants, rain and wind, mountains, waves, liquor, a door, a helmet, armor, spraying blood, a bow or a cane. In some cases, the fan is replaced with a real flag, drinking glass or cane, but it is generally possible to express all these things with a sword or a fan.

さまざまな「扇の見立て」

徳利で酒を注ぐ
Filling a cup with sake from a bottle

大盃で酒を飲む
Drinking sake from a cup

手紙を書く
Writing a letter

書を読む
Reading

戸を開ける
Opening a door

舟を漕ぐ
Rowing a boat

舟の棹をさす
Poling a boat

太鼓を打つ
Beating a drum

琵琶を弾く
Playing a biwa
(Japanese lute)

笛を吹く
Playing a flute

鼓を打つ
Beating a hand drum

兜
Helmet

笠
Bamboo hat

槍を構える
Holding a spear

弓を引く
Drawing a bow

流れる雲
Passing cloud

風
Wind

さざ波
Rippling waves

荒波
Raging waves

散り花
Scattering blossoms

（小刻みに揺らすと）雨
（はらはらと揺らすと）雪

Short and quick movements: **rain**
Long and slow movements: **snow**

日の出
Sunrise

山から月が出る
Moonrise

■流派による表現の違いも見どころ

ところで、同じ物を表すにも、流派によってどこまで写実的に表すか、どこまでデフォルメするのか、あるいはどの部分を扇子で表し、どの部分を反対の手や仕草で表すかなど、考え方の違いで、見立ての型が変わってきます。一つの例として、「弓矢の見立て」について、二つの流派の所作を紹介しましょう。

正賀流の弓の見立てでは、左手で扇を縦に構え、右手はこぶしで弓を引きます。そして右腕を垂直に上げることで矢を放ちます。一方、小天真道流の弓の見立ては、左手で扇を縦に構えるのは同じですが、左手は四指を揃えて矢を引きます。そして右腕を斜め上に上げて矢を放ちます。この時に左手は手首を内に返して、扇を寝かせます。正賀流の所作よりも、より写実的な表現といえるで

Main differences between the expressive styles of different schools

Depending on the school, there are different ideas as to how realistically something should be expressed; to what extent things should be deformed; what parts should be expressed with a folding fan, and what parts are better communicated using the other hand or body movements to express one and the same thing. Accordingly, each school teaches different mitate patterns. Below is a graphic explanation of two different schools' postures for expressing a bow and arrow.

The Seiga-ryu does this by holding a fan vertically with the left hand, and using the fist of the right hand to imitate the drawing of the bow. Moving the right arm straight up expresses the release of the bow.

A fan held vertically in the left hand is also how the Shotenshindo-ryu expresses a bow, however here the arrow is pulled

しょう。

しかし、背筋を真っ直ぐ伸ばし、肘をしっかり張り、指先まで整え、目線の高さを安定させることなどはどちらの流派も共通しており、同じ剣舞というフィールドにおいてそれぞれの流儀が形づくられてきたことが伺えます。なお、これらの所作は決して固定されたものではなく、作品によって変わることがあります。

このように、流派による違いを発見することも、舞台を観る楽しみの一つです。

小天真道流の「弓の見立て」

using four fingers of the right hand, and released by moving the right arm diagonally upward. The wrist of the left hand is now bent inwards, so that the fan is in a horizontal position. Compared to the Seiga-ryu, it is certainly an overall more realistic representation.

What both schools share is the upright posture with back muscles straightened, elbows squared, hands and fingers set in position, and the gaze steadily fixed at a certain height. From here one can observe how each school has worked out its own distinctive style within the field of kenbu. The postures described above are not necessarily completely fixed, but may vary by performance.

Discovering such differences between different schools is also part of the fun of watching a performance.

3 演者の気迫を体感する

ここまで、「詩文の予習」と「表現方法を知る」ことが舞台を楽しむために必要と述べましたが、この二つを勉強するには、かなりの時間と努力が必要になります。実際のところ、それを実践しなくても気にすることなく、機会があるなら、まずは舞台会場まで足を運んでみましょう。知識はなくとも、吟士の吟声、そして演者の気迫と力強さを舞台で味わいましょう。演舞を観て、振りや表現を楽しみ、歴史ロマンや侍の生き様に思いを馳せるようになれれば、あなたも立派な剣舞ファンです。

3 Spirit of the performer

I mentioned above that "preliminary research on poetry" and "knowledge of means of expression" are necessary for the enjoyment of kenbu, but both of these take a significant amount of time and effort. As a matter of fact, there is no need to worry even without such preparation. If you have the chance, I would recommend to go and pay a visit to a kenbu venue, and experience first-hand the recitalist's voice and the performer's spirit and vigor, even without prior knowledge. Watch the dance, enjoy the gestures and expressions, let your thoughts travel back through history to the romantic time of the samurai, and you will soon be a magnificent kenbu fan.

武士の歴史と剣舞演目

剣舞の題材となる漢詩や和歌などの詩歌には、武士が詠み手となるものが多く含まれます。「武士」がどのような人々であったのか、その歴史や考え方を知ることで、詩をより深く理解することができるでしょう。

■武士と侍は同じ?

侍とは、そばで見守り待機することを意味する「さぶらう」を語源とし、平安時代は貴族と凡下（一般庶民）の間に位置する身分を指しました。身分＝職業というわけではないので、侍の中には戦うことを生業とする武士の他に、少数の文士（学問・儒学・文学などの仕事に携わる人）も存在しました。ただ、数の面で武士が圧倒的

だったため、次第に侍＝武士というイメージが定着し、十五世紀後半の戦国期までには実際にほぼイコールで捉えられるようになったと考えられます。

■武士はどこからやってきたか

近年、武士に関する歴史研究が著しく進んでいます。かつては、武士は東方（都のある奈良や京から見て、東に位置する現在の関東地方や東北地方）の農村で荘園の警護する者として誕生し、やがて都で貴族を上回る力をつけて独自の政権を作るに至ったと学校で教えられていましたが、現在は、武士は都市の中から生まれたと考えるようになっています。

Kenbu programs and the history of the samurai

Many of the Chinese or waka poems that kenbu programs are themed on were composed by samurai. Knowing more about samurai – what kind of people they were, their history and philosophy – will help you gain a deeper understanding of their poems.

Is 武士 the same as 侍?

The term "samurai" (侍) is derived from the verb "saburau," the literal meaning of which is "to watch (someone) and wait," or "to serve." In the Heian period, the social position of the samurai was between the aristocracy and the common people. As "position" is not equal to "profession," there were samurai whose main occupation was to fight, but also a few "literary men" who were involved with academic work, Confucian studies or literature. Numerically, however, there were far more 武士 (bushi), so the images of 武士 and 侍 gradually coalesced into a single "samurai" image. In the sengoku era of civil wars in the second half of the 15th century, the distinction between 武士 and 侍 virtually disappeared.

貴族社会と平家の台頭

武士が力を持ち始めるのは十世紀中頃以降です。天皇の子に氏姓を与えて臣籍降下させる政策が取られ、のちに武士の大集団をつくる源氏・平氏が生まれました。両氏は天皇の命令を受けて地方の平定に出かけては武功を競い、互いに切磋琢磨しながら勢力を拡大していきます。

平安後期、朝廷で王家内部の対立や寺院間の競合が激しくなります。武力紛争にも発展し、都の皇族・貴族たちの間で武士の存在感が増します。平家の平清盛は、圧倒的な軍事力を背景に政治勢力を増し、太政大臣に昇進、政略結婚により天皇の外祖父にまで上り詰めます。

遙かに籠背を観れば　一蓬莱／靄靄たる雲煙　瑞臺を擁す／月は長廊に落ち
灣上静かなり／萬燈の星列　波を照らして來る —— 浅野坤山「厳島」

飛鳥時代に建立された世界遺産・厳島神社は、源平時代に平清盛による大規模な改修が行われ、平家の守り神社となった。

（図版：宮島祭礼図屏風　東京国立博物館蔵）

Itsukushima Shrine, a world heritage site established in the Asuka period, was extensively repaired by Taira no Kiyomori in the Gempei period, and became the patron shrine of the Taira clan."

東風吹かば　匂いおこせよ
梅の花　主なしとて　春な
忘るな ── 菅原道真『拾遺
集』

政敵の策略で京から九州の
大宰府へ左遷されることに
なった菅原道真は、日ごろ
愛していた梅の木に別れを
告げる。（図版：月百姿
月輝如晴雪梅花似照星可憐
金鏡転庭上玉房馨　菅原道
真　国立国会図書館蔵）

Demoted as Dazaifu from Kyoto
to Kyushu as a strategic measure
of the political opponent,
Sugawara no Michizane bids
farewell to the plum trees that he
loved so much. "You plum
blossoms! Even though you lose
your master, don't be oblivious
to spring.""

The history of the samurai (1)
Aristocratic society and the rise of the Heike

The samurai first gained power in the middle of the 10th century. They took such measures as giving the emperor's children lineage and hereditary titles, and making them renounce imperial privileges, before the Taira and Minamoto families formed large samurai clans. Both clans received orders from the emperor, rendered distinguished military services by subjugating the rural areas, and expanded their powers through a friendly rivalry.

In the late Heian period, conflicts within the imperial family and the rivalry between temples intensified and developed into armed disputes, resulting in an increased presence of samurai in both royalty and aristocracy in the capital. On the foundation of overwhelming military power, Taira no Kiyomori of the Heike family gained also increased political influence. He was promoted to Daijo-daijin (Grand Minister), and through his political marriage eventually became the emperor's maternal grandfather.

［武士の歴史②］
源平合戦と鎌倉幕府

　一方、源氏の源頼朝は、幼年の頃の戦で平家に敗れ、東方（伊豆国）に流されますが、平家政権に不満を持つ地方の武士をまとめ、鎌倉を本拠地として東国での地位を確かなものとします。

　頼朝は弟の義経を平家追討のため西に派遣し、一の谷の戦い、屋島の戦いと平家を追い詰め、ついには一一八五年、壇ノ浦の戦いで平家を滅亡させます。源頼朝は天皇から「征夷大将軍」（武士の頂点に立つ者に与えられる称号）に任ぜられ、以降、武家による政権（「幕府」）という呼称が明治期に付けられた）が、明治期まで続くことになります。

源義経（『大日本歴史錦繪』より）国立国会図書館蔵

The history of the samurai (2)
The Genpei War and the Kamakura Shogunate

Minamoto no Yoritomo from the Genji clan, on the other hand, was sent to the eastern Izu country following defeat through the Heike during his childhood. Based in Kamakura, he gathered a group of local samurai that were dissatisfied with the Heike administration around him, and solidified his position in the east. Yoritomo dispatched his brother Yoshitsune to the west in order to hunt down the Heike family, and after cornering the Heike in the battles at Ichinotani and Yashima, they finally managed to extinguish the Heike clan in the battle at Dannoura in 1185. Minamoto no Yoritomo was appointed as Seii Taishogun (a degree that indicates the highest samurai position) by the emperor, after which the samurai administration continued until the Meiji period (when the system was called bakufu).

一の谷の軍営　遂に支えず／平家の末路　人をして悲しましむ／戦雲収まる処　残月有り／塞上笛は哀し　吹きし者は誰ぞ —— 松口月城「青葉の笛」

栄華を極めた平家一族であったが、源氏の猛攻により、遂に滅亡のときを迎える。「一の谷の合戦」で、平家の若き武将・平敦盛が敵に背中を向けたところ、背後から呼び止められた。（図版：勝川春章　敦盛直実　東京国立博物館蔵　Image: TNM Image Archives）

After decades of prosperity, the Taira clan is eventually brought to extinction as a result of the Minamoto clan's attacks. "The Battle at Ichinotani" depicts a scene in which the young general Taira no Atsumori is stopped by the enemy he had turned his back to.

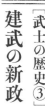

鎌倉幕府は約一五〇年間存続しますが、一三三三年、後醍醐天皇が天皇みずからが政治をおこなう親政を理想とし、幕府に不満を持つ武士を集めて挙兵し、鎌倉幕府を倒します。後醍醐天皇は新政権を樹立（建武の新政）しますが、三

天莫空勾践　時非無范蠡
てんこうせんをむなしゅうすることなかれ ときにはんれいなきにしもあらず
―― 児島高徳 『太平記』

後醍醐天皇の家臣・児島高徳は、隠岐に流されることになった天皇を奪還しようと、夜に行在所に忍び込むも、厳重な警備に断念する。桜の幹に「いつかきっと、忠義な家臣が出現いたします」という意味の中国の故事に基づいた漢詩を書いた。（図版：児島備後三郎（児島高徳）図　東京国立博物館蔵）

In order to rescue Emperor Godaigo, who was exiled to the Oki Islands, his retainer Kojima Takanori attempted to sneak into the emperor's temporary residence at night, but eventually gave up as the place was heavily guarded. The poem he composed by a cherry tree is an allusion to a Chinese historical event, meaning "a loyal retainer will surely appear someday."

沙汀南望すれば　煙波浩たり／聞くならく三軍
此れ自り過ぐと／潮水帰来して　人事改まり／空
山迢遰　夕陽多し──太宰春台「稲叢懐古」

武将・新田義貞が稲村ケ崎にて黄金作りの太刀を
海に投じたところ、龍神が呼応して潮が引き、鎌
倉に攻め入ることができたという伝説がある。（図
版：新田義貞稲村ヶ崎にて太刀を海中に投ず　東
京都立図書館蔵）

According to legend, when general Nitta Yoshisada cast his
gold ornamented sword into the sea at Inamuragasaki, the
dragon god responded by making the tide go out and
thereby open the way for Nitta to invade Kamakura. "

年もしないうちに、源氏一族
の足利尊氏が後醍醐天皇を幽
閉し（後に吉野に脱出）、別の天
皇を立てた上で、征夷大将軍
に就任、室町幕府を発足させ
ました。

The history of the samurai (3)
From the new Kenmu administration to the Muromachi Bakufu

The Kamakura bakufu continued for about 150 years, until in 1333, emperor Godaigo raised an army of samurai who were
dissatisfied with the bakufu, and overthrew the Kamakura bakufu, according to his idea of a direct imperial government
with the emperor himself engaging in politics. Emperor Godaigo established a new government (the new Kenmu
administration), but after less than three years, Ashikaga Takauji from the Genji clan put emperor Godaigo under arrest
(although he later escaped to Yoshino), installed a new emperor, and launched the Muromachi bakufu in his position as
Seii Taishogun.

室町時代の文化

京都を拠点に政権を担った足利氏は、伝統的な公家文化や大陸から伝わった禅宗を積極的に取り入れ、能、茶道、庭園、建築、連歌など、今日まで続く多様な日本文化・芸術が花開きました。これらは経済力をつけた庶民にも浸透し、さらに十一年も続いた応仁の乱で地方に散った公家や僧侶を通じて地方にも広がることになりました〈小京都〉。

碧海の中央　六里の松／天橋の絶景　是仙蹤／夜深くして　人は龍燈の出ずるを待つ／月は落ち　文殊堂裏の鐘 —— 釈希世「天の橋立」

厳島、天の橋立、松島と併せて古来「日本三景」と呼ばれている。様々な文化が花開いた室町時代においても、これらを讃える多くの絵画作品や詩歌が生まれた。（図版：『日本国宝全集.第59輯』より天橋立図　国会図書館蔵）

Itsukushima, Amanohashidate and Matsushima are known as "the three beauty spots of Japan" since ancient times. Numerous paintings and poems were made in praise of these places especially in the Muromachi period, an era of various blossoming cultural activities.

The history of the samurai (4)
The culture of the Muromachi era

Ashikaga headed the government from his base in Kyoto, and actively embraced the traditional culture of court nobles, as well as Zen Buddhism that had been brought to Japan from the Asian continent. Noh, tea ceremony, gardening, architecture, renga (linked poems) and various other forms of Japanese art and culture that are still alive today particularly flourished around that time. They also spread among common people who had acquired economic power, and through courtiers and priests that were scattered across the country in the 11-year-long Onin War, they were further dispersed also in the rural areas. (See also "Sho-Kyoto" or "little Kyoto").

東山殿猿楽興行図　東京都立図書館蔵

［武士の歴史⑤］

戦国期

本能寺焼討之圖

織田信長

十五世紀半ばから、地方の守護大名が幕府の統制から離脱する動きが活発になり、室町幕府の中央政権としての機能が失われてゆきます。守護大名を倒して新たな大名となる者も続出し、それぞれが同盟関係を結んだり合戦を繰り広げたりしながら領国拡大を目指しました。歴史に名

を残す有力な戦国大名が多数生まれますが、その中で、尾張国の織田信長が室町将軍を追放して天下人の地位を得ます。織田は本能寺の変で倒れてしまいますが、織田の家臣であった豊臣秀吉が天下統一を果たし、豊臣政権を樹立します。

本能寺　溝の深さ　幾尺なるぞ／吾れ大事を就すは　今夕に在り／茭粽手に在り　茭を併せて食ろう／四簷の梅雨　天墨の如し――頼山陽「本能寺」抜粋

天下統一を果たした織田信長であったが、家臣の明智光秀の謀反により滞在先の本能寺で死を遂げた。「本能寺の溝の深さは一体どのくらいあるのだろうか、その本能寺にいる信長を撃つのは今夕が好機である。」（図版：本能寺焼討之図　東京都立図書館蔵）

After having accomplished the unification of Japan, Oda Nobunaga died at Honno-ji as a result of his retainer Akechi Mitsuhide's rebellious attack. "I wonder how deep the ditch at Honno-ji is. Nobunaga stays at Honno-ji tonight, so this is a good chance to attack."

The history of the samurai (5)
The Sengoku era

From the middle of the 15th century, the trend of local shugo daimyo (feudal lords) seceding from the control of the bakufu gained momentum, and the Muromachi bakufu was gradually deprived of its central government function. Cases in which the local shugo daimyo was overthrown by individuals who then became the new daimyo occurred one after another, and through alliances and repeated battles these new daimyo aimed to expand their territory. That time produced numerous influential warlords that went on to make history. One of them, Oda Nobunaga from Owari Province, banished the Muromachi shoguns, and acquired a ruling position. Oda eventually died in the Honno-ji incident, and it was his former retainer Toyotomi Hideyoshi who accomplished the country's unification, and established the Toyotomi administration.

関ヶ原の合戦〜江戸幕府

豊臣秀吉の死後、跡継ぎである嫡男・豊臣秀頼が幼かったことから、家臣の徳川家康が実権を握り始め、豊臣家を守ろうとする石田三成らの勢力と対立します。一六〇〇年、関ヶ原の戦いにおいて、徳川は勝利し、一六〇三年に征夷大将軍を任命され、以後約二五〇年に渡る江戸幕府が始まりました。

江戸幕府は、外国との交易を制限することで内政に集中し、強固な支配を続けることに成功しました。一七二一年の人口調査で、江戸の町人人口は五十万人を超え、これに武家や寺社の人口を含めると百万人に近いとも言われています。一八〇一年のロンドンの人口が八十六万人、パリが五十四万人だそうですから、江戸が世界トップクラスの人口を持つ大都市であったことが分かります。

The history of the samurai (6)
From the battle of Sekigahara to the Edo Shogunate

When Toyotomi Hideyoshi died, his heir and successor Toyotomi Hideyori was still a little boy. Toyotomi's retainer Tokugawa Ieyasu eventually began to seize real power, which brought him into collision with Ishida Mitsunari, whose interest it was to protect the Toyotomi clan. Tokugawa won the battle of Sekigahara in 1600, and was appointed Seii Taishogun in 1603, which marked the beginning of the Edo shogunate that lasted for approximately 250 years.

Limiting trade with other countries allowed the Edo shogunate to focus on domestic politics, and thereby solidify its sustained power. According to a population survey conducted in 1721, the population of townspeople in Edo exceeded 500,000, and it is said that, when including the samurai and clerical population as well, the total number was close to one million. Considering that the population of London in 1801 was 860,000, and that of Paris 540,000, one understands that Edo was in the top class of international big cities in terms of population.

水戸光圀公之肖像

蒼龍 猶ほ未だ雲霄に昇らず／潜んで 神州 剣客の腰に在り／髯虜 甕せんと欲すれば策無きに非ず／容易に汚す勿れ 日本刀 ── 徳川光圀「日本刀を詠ず」

水戸黄門の名でも知られる徳川光圀は、江戸時代の初期〜中期にあって、儒学思想を中心に、国学・史学・神道を結合させたし政治思想の学問「水戸学」の基礎を作った。水戸学は、全国の武家の子息が通う藩校で教えられ、幕末まで大きな影響力を与えた。（図版：水戸光圀（『水戸光圀公之肖像及書』より） 京都大学附属図書館蔵）

Tokugawa Mitsukuni, also known by the name Mito Komon, laid the foundation for the politically inspired "Mitogaku," based around the philosophy of Confucianism and integrating studies of Japanese classical literature, history and the Shinto religion, in the early to mid Edo period. A highly influential science up to the late Tokugawa period, Mitogaku was was taught nationwide at schools where the sons of samurai families were enrolled.

開国と江戸幕府の終焉

江戸後期になると、資本主義列強の外国船が日本に来航し、開国を迫ります。米ペリー艦隊の黒船に代表される圧倒的な軍事力差を前に、幕府は和親条約を結び開国します。

江戸幕府は軍事改革に着手し、西洋式の武器を取り入れ、西洋式の軍隊制度を模倣しようとします。しかし、もともと軍事政権である徳川政権において軍制を変えようとすることは、従来の身分制度や政治体制の根本を否定することになるため、結局全面的な改革に踏み切れずに失敗する運命にありました。

幕府に見切りを付けた薩摩や長州といった地方の武士が独自に軍団を作り、幾度もの戦乱と和議を重ねながら幕府を追い詰めます。一八六七年、ついに十五代将軍・徳川慶喜が二条城で政権を天皇に返還することを宣言し（大政奉還）、江戸城を明け渡すことになりました。これをもって、約七〇〇年続いた武士支配が幕を閉じました。

The history of the samurai (7)
The opening of the country and the demise of the Edo Sho-gunate
Toward the end of the Edo period, the foreign ships of the capitalist great powers arrived in Japan, and pressed the country to open up. In the face of the overwhelming difference in military power as represented by American Commodore Perry's kurofune (black ships), the shogunate signed a treaty of peace and amity, and eventually opened the country.
The Edo shogunate quickly started working on a military reform, incorporated western-style arms, and tried to imitate western military systems. However, as the attempt to change the military system of the Tokugawa administration, which was a military regime in the first place, meant to deny the existing class system and the principles of the political system at large, the project was doomed to failure, and an all-out reform could not be undertaken.
Local samurai in the Satsuma or Choshu regions who had given up on the shogunate put together their own armies, and eventually brought the shogunate to bay through repeated wars and peace conferences. In 1867, the 15th shogun Tokugawa Yoshinobu finally announced at Nijo Castle the return of the political power to the emperor (see also "restoration of imperial rule"), which led to the handover of Edo Castle. This marked at once the end of the rule of the samurai that had continued for about 700 years.

吾　今　国の為に死す／死して君親に背か
ず／悠々たり天地の事／鑑照明神に在り
——吉田松陰「辞世」

武士で教育者であった吉田松陰は、２９歳
で江戸幕府により斬首刑とされるも、のち
の明治維新で活躍する若い武士に大きな思
想的な影響を与えた。（図版：吉田松陰　国
立国会図書館蔵）

Samurai and educator Yoshida Shoin was sentenced
to death by decapitation by the Edo shogunate at the
age of 29, and went on to exert a major ideological
influence on the young samurai that were active
during the following Meiji restoration.

南鶴城を望めば　砲煙あがる／痛哭　涙を
飲んで　且つ彷徨す／宗社亡びぬ　我が事
畢る／十有六人　屠腹して僵る——佐原
盛純「白虎隊」抜粋

明治元年の戊辰戦争の時、会津藩に忠誠を
誓う少年たちは「白虎隊」と名乗り、会津
城を守ろうとした。しかし戦いに利なく、
最後は飯盛山で自刃して悲劇的に散った。
（図版：白虎隊　会津若松市蔵）

At the time of the Boshin War in 1868, young men
who had pledged allegiance to the Aizu feudal clan
formed a group called "Byakkotai" to protect Aizu
Castle. However their operations failed, and
eventually ended tragically with the members'
suicide at Mt. Iimoriyama.

武士の価値観・精神性とは？

儒教を取り入れた治者の倫理

ここまで武士の政治史を主に見てきましたが、ここからは、武士がどんな存在だったのかを考えてみましょう。

多くの日本人にとって、武士は単なる野蛮な戦士ではなく、倫理的・道徳的な存在としても見ているのではないかと思います。これは、江戸幕府が十七世紀後半から文治政治に転換し、徳川の平和（Pax Tokugawa）が実現した影響によるものです。

戦国期以前は、武士の生き様は「ツワモノの道」、「弓矢取る身の習い」などという表現が使われ、死への覚悟が武士の自己鍛錬の中で大き

な比重を占めていました。それが、江戸期に入ると、武士はそれぞれが徳川政権における役割を与えられ、個々の軍事集団としての機能は凍結されました。その上で、戦士としての気風・心がけを守ると同時に、人心を引きつける指導者としての道徳心を身に着けることが必要とされました。

江戸幕府は、ほんらい「武」の対立物である「儒教」を武士の治者としての自覚をうながす教養体系として取り入れます。儒教から言葉や考え方を借りてくることによって、為政者として自分を厳しく律し、心が

Samurai values and mentality

Ruler ethics incorporating elements of Confucianism

Following the above introduction with a focus on the political history of samurai, I will now talk about what kind of person a samurai was.

I suppose that many Japanese see a samurai not simply as a barbaric soldier, but also as a person of morals and ethics. This has much to do with the transformation of the Edo shogunate into a civilian government, and the implementation of the Pax Tokugawa in the late 17th century.

Up to the Sengoku era, the lifestyle of a samurai had been referred to as that of a "warrior with bow and arrow," whereas the readiness to die occupied a large percentage within the ascetic practices of a samurai. Upon entering the Edo period, the samurai were given roles as part of the Tokugawa administration, and the functions of their respective individual military groups were put on ice. In addition, while retaining their warrior character and attitude, they were also required to develop the moral sense of a leader who is able to attract people.

The Edo shogunate incorporated Confucianism, the polar opposite of armed fight, as an educational system that encourages a samurai's consciousness as a ruler. Samurai were instructed to borrow expressions and ideas from Confucianism that help them to strictly restrain themselves as policymakers, and straighten their attitudes and behaviors. In "Yamaga Gorui," established in 1663, military strategist and Confucianist Yamaga Soko suggests that "a samurai should set an example by showing wellmannered behavior in all his movements." Furthermore, Yamaga's disciple Daidoji Yuzan argues in "Budo Shoshinshu (The Code of the Samurai)" (1716-36) that, "Above all else, the samurai must be firmly resolved that he can die anytime, day or night, from the time he eats his zoni soup on the morning of the first day of the new year until the night of the last day of the year. [...] Loyalty, justice and valor are most essential to Bushido. The samurai possessed of these three virtues is the most outstanding example thereof."

けや振る舞いを正すよう指導しました。

兵学者であり儒者である山鹿素行は、一六六三年に成立した『山鹿語類』で、武士に対して「日々の一挙手一投足にいたるまで、作法に適った立ち振る舞いを行い、手本を見せるべき」だと諭しています。また、山鹿素行の弟子である大道寺友山は、『武道初心集』（一七一六～三六年成立）で、「武士たるもの、元日の朝から大晦日の夜に至るまで日々夜々、常時死を心がけるをもって本望であり、忠、義、勇の三つを兼ね備えたものが最高の武士だ」と説いています。

ことわざに見る
理想の武士像

こうした武士の考え方や立ち振る舞いの有り様は、江戸時代の庶民が楽しんだ歌舞伎や浄瑠璃、文楽の作品中にも登場し、いくつかは俚諺（りげん）（ことわざ）にもなっています。

「武士に二言なし」

「武士は情を知る」

「武士は食わねど高楊枝」

これらは、庶民の間で共有されてきた武士像であり、「かくあるべし」と期待する姿だともいえます。全ての武士がこのように素晴らしい徳を備えた人々だったということではな

いでしょうし、実際には大きく隔たりがあることでしょう。ただ重要なのは、この「あるべき姿」が庶民に共有され、庶民からそのように振る舞うことが期待されていたことが、武士自身、自らの身を律することに繋がっていたのではないかと思います。

そして、剣舞を含む多くの芸能作品に武士の「あるべき姿」が示され、芸能を通して、今も国内外の人々に発信され続けているのです。

The ideal samurai as depicted in proverbs

Such kind of samurai thinking and acting was incorporated also into Kabuki, Joruri or Bunraku performances that were popular with the common people in the Edo period, and expressed in several proverbs.

A samurai never goes back on his word.

A samurai knows mercy.

A samurai uses a toothpick even when he has nothing to eat.

These proverbs reflect an image of the samurai that has become common among the general public, and at once certainly also a certain expectation as to "how they are supposed be." But not all samurai were necessarily such magnificent people of great virtue, and as a matter of fact, there must have been big differences between them. What is essential, however, is that this common idea of "how they are supposed be," and the expectations as to how a samurai should behave, have certainly inspired the samurai to square themselves accordingly. This image of the "ideal samurai" has been projected in numerous pieces of performing arts including kenbu, and it is still being communicated to people in and outside Japan through performing arts.

『Bushido — the soul of Japan』

ところで、武士はいつからこれほど世界的に知られるようになったのでしょうか。武士が特に倫理的な存在として広く知られることになった一つのきっかけに、新渡戸稲造著『Bushido — The Soul of Japan』（武士道）があります。明治三十三年に英語で著された同著は、数年のうちにドイツ語、ポーランド語、フランス語、ノルウェー語、ハンガリー語、ロシア語、イタリア語に翻訳され、世界的なベストセラーになりました。教育者として幅広く活躍し、国際連盟事務次長も務めた新渡戸は大変尊敬に値する人で、『Bushido』は侍に興味を持つ多くの人が一度は読んでいるだろう点で古典だといえます。まだ読んだことがない方は、ぜ

新渡戸稲造『Bushido - the soul of Japan』明治33年、盛岡市先人記念館提供

Nitobe Inazo "Bushido – The Soul of Japan"

ひ手に取ってみてほしいと思います。

ただ、「武士道」という言葉が江戸期以前に普及した用語だったかといえばそうではなく、歴史学者の間では、『Bushido』の評価はそれほど高いとはいえません。『Bushido』があくまで、明治の半ばを過ぎてから、歴史専門家ではない人物が著したものであることには気をつけておきましょう。

"Bushido – The Soul of Japan"

Since about when do the samurai enjoy such a degree of familiarity around the world? One occasion that widely introduced the concept of samurai especially as persons of ethical behavior was the publication of Nitobe Inazo's book "Bushido - The Soul of Japan." Originally written in English in 1900, within a few years the book was translated into German, Polish, French, Norwegian, Hungarian, Russian and Italian, and became an international bestseller. Nitobe was a widely active educator, and at once also UnderSecretary General of the League of Nations. He was a man who deserved great esteem and respect, and considering that "Bushido" is one book that everyone with an interest in samurai culture has probably read at least once, it is definitely a classic. If you haven't read it yet, I do recommend to pick it up when you have the chance.

The term "bushido" however is not an expression that was popular before the Edo period, and among historians, the book "Bushido" doesn't enjoy a particularly high reputation. After all, we should bear in mind that "Bushido" was written in the second half of the Meiji era, by a person who was not an expert in the field of history.

詩吟について

第一章の最後に、詩吟について触れておきましょう。古典的な剣舞は詩吟なくして成立しえません。詩吟とは漢詩を吟ずることをいい、「吟詠」とほぼ同義です。日本における漢詩の受容と、現代詩吟への道程を紹介します。

漢詩の伝来と発展

日本へは六〇〇年から始まった遣隋使・遣唐使により伝わったとされ、七五一年には日本最古の漢詩集といわれる『懐風藻』が編纂されました。日本漢詩の隆盛の頂点は、江戸期から明治初期にかけてで、「文人」と呼ばれる多くの詩人が輩出されました。

漢詩を吟じること

では、この漢詩を吟じるという文化はどこから生まれたのでしょうか。

一つには、平安朝時代に貴族社会で流行した「朗詠」が挙げられます。ただ、これが詩吟の直接のルーツとはいえません。

詩吟が生まれるきっかけになったのは、江戸中期、徳川五代将軍・綱吉の時代です。昌平坂学問所が設立され、漢詩の講義において、学生たちの興味を引くために漢詩に「節」をつけて読んで聞かせたのが始まりとされています。次いで、文化・文政期（一八〇四～一八三〇年）には、広瀬淡窓が主宰する学問所でも同様のことが行われ、次第に他の私塾や各地の藩校に広がったとするのが定説になっています。

幕末の志士は、悲憤慷慨を表現するため、好んで詩を吟じたといわれます。彼らの漢詩は、剣舞の作品としても多く取り上げられています。

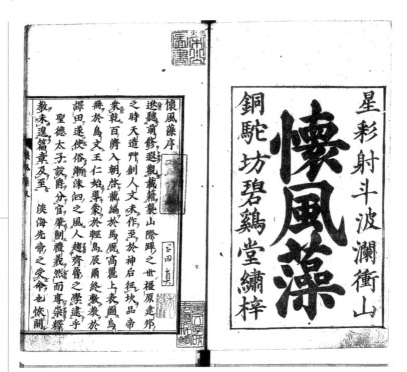

日本最古の漢詩集『懐風藻』江戸期の復刻本
版元 長尾平兵衛、1684（天和4）年、国文学研究資料館蔵

Edo period edition of "Kaifuso," the oldest collection of Chinese poems in Japan

Poetry recitation

Let me close the first chapter by explaining a little more about poetry recitation (*shigin*). The recitation of poems is an integral part without which there would be no kenbu. *Shigin* is the term that is used to refer to recitation of classical Chinese poems in particular, and it is virtually synonymous with ginei. Below I will talk about the reception of classical Chinese poetry in Japan, and the process toward modern recitation styles.

The introduction and expansion of classical Chinese poetry in Japan

It is said that classical Chinese poetry was introduced to Japan with the Japanese missions to Sui and Tang China that began in the year 600. "Kaifuso," the oldest collection of Chinese poems in Japan, was compiled in 751. When Chinese-style poetry was at the height of prosperity in Japan between the Edo and the early Meiji period, a number of poets emerged that came to be known as "bunjin."

現代の詩吟

明治期以降、詩吟は剣舞の広がりと同様に各地で流派が作られ、習い事の一つとして広まっていきます。特に、昭和とともに始まったラジオ放送は吟詠に大きな啓蒙を与えました。

戦時下では国威高揚に資するものとして奨励され世間に広がりましたが、戦後は古今の名詩を味わい、美しい日本語をもって表現するといった芸術性が前面に出されるようにな

りました。

なお、かつてCDやテープがなかった時代は、お稽古や舞台で生吟詠（「地吟」という）で剣舞が舞われており、そのため、どの剣舞流派でも詩吟の稽古が並行して行われていました。

現在は詩吟が挿入されたCDやテープが多く発売されているため、舞だけを指導する流派も多数存在します。

The recitation of classical Chinese poems

Now where does this culture of reciting Chinese poems originate from? Even though it cannot be considered to represent the direct roots of shigin, one point of origin is certainly the fashion of "recitation" (roei) that prevailed in the aristocratic circles in the Heian period.

An occasion that inspired the birth of shigin rather directly came with the inauguration of the fifth Tokugawa Shogun Tsunayoshi around the middle of the Edo period. At the newly established Shoheizaka school (the predecessor of today's University of Tokyo) poems were read to the students with added "melodies" in order to attract the students' interest in lectures on classical Chinese poetry. During the civil administration period 1804-1830, similar lessons were also offered at Hirose Tanso's Kangien school, and according to an established theory, the practice then spread to other private and local domain schools.

Patriots in the late Tokugawa period are also said to have favored poetry recitation as a means for expressing their indignation. Many of their Chinese-style poems have been featured also in kenbu performances.

詩道楠水吟詠会　松葉実水氏

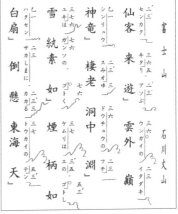

詩吟の教本の一例『吟道瑞鳳流教本』より
瑞鳳流提供

Textbook instructions (example) for the shigin performance of "Fujisan"

Poetry recitation today

Since the Meiji era, just like in the case of kenbu, the fashion of poetry recitation resulted in the establishment of various local schools across the country, and recitation became popular as a subject that was taught in lessons. It was especially also the start of radio broadcasts in the Showa era that had a greatly illuminating effect of the recitation of poetry.

During the war, poetry recitation was recommended and popularized as something that - together with uplifting music - helps raise national prestige, and after the war, the artistic side of poetry came to be highlighted through the enjoyment of famous poems and their expression through beautiful Japanese language.

In an age when CDs and cassette tapes did not yet exist, in lessons and performances kenbu was accompanied by live poetry recitation, and thus lessons in poetry reading were offered concurrently across the different schools. As a variety of CDs and tapes of poetry recitals are available today, many schools focus on teaching the dance parts only.

世界の剣舞

剣を使って舞う文化は世界各地にあります。そのいくつかを紹介します。

韓国の剣舞（コンム）

女性二〜八名がそれぞれ二本の刀を手にし、音楽に合わせてフォーメーションを変えながら舞うもの。高麗時代（九一八〜一三九二頃）に中国の妓女制度が取り入れられ、妓生（キーセン）と呼ばれる歌舞を専門とする女性を育成して、宮中舞踊としてその後の李氏朝鮮時代（一三九二〜一九一〇年）まで活躍しました。現在も伝統舞踊として継承され、中でも晋州剣舞（チンジュコンム）は韓国の重要無形文化財に指定されています。

トルコの剣舞「クルチュ・カルカン」

クルチュは剣、カルカンは盾を意味し、トルコ第四の都市ブルサに伝わる民族舞踊です。オスマンによる統治、支配の様子を剣と盾を使用して表現します。元は、トルコ兵の兵士が剣術の鍛錬のために行っていた訓練が民衆の踊りに取り込まれたもので、オスマン初期の軍服を着用し、舞い手が剣と盾でたてる金属音に合わせて踊ります。今もフェスティバルなどで披露されています。

Sword dance around the world

There exist cultures and traditions that involve dancing with swords in countries around the world. Below are a few examples.

Korean sword dance (kummu)

This dance is performed to music and in varying formations by groups of two to eight women, each carrying two swords. After the Chinese system of official dancers was implemented also in Korea in the Goryeo period (ca. 918-1392), so-called kisaeng – women specializing in song and dance – were trained to perform kummu as a form of court dance throughout the following era of Korean dynasties (1392-1910). The tradition is still being kept alive today, and such variants as "Jinju Kummu" have been designated as important intangible cultural heritage of Korea.

Turkish sword dance "Kılıç Kalkan"

Combining the words "kılıç" (sword) and "kalkan" (shield), this folk dance originated in Bursa, the city with the

中国の剣舞

中国において剣舞というと、「鴻門の会」が頭に浮かぶことでしょう。紀元前二〇六年、西楚の覇王・項羽と、後に前漢の初代皇帝となる劉邦の和解会談において、項羽側の武将・范増（はんぞう）が部下の項荘に命じ余興の剣舞を披露しながら劉邦に斬りかかろうとし、その企みに気づいた項羽の叔父・項伯（こうはく）が相方として剣舞を舞い、范増の攻撃を阻止したという事件です。この事件で両者の信頼関係

構築は失敗に終わり、楚漢戦争が勃発、項羽は敗北し、劉邦は前漢の初代皇帝となりました。この故事は中国を代表する民族芸能である「京劇」の演目にもなっています。

漢代以降、剣は権力と地位を象徴するものとして宮廷舞踊に取り入れられ、武術の立ち姿、姿勢、型を学ぶための訓練方法としても活用されました。

fourth highest population in Turkey. The dance illustrates the rule and governance of the Ottomans using a sword and a shield. Originally a training method of the Turkish soldiers to hone their fencing skills, their practice was incorporated into popular dance. "Kılıç Kalkan" is performed in military uniforms from the early days of the Ottoman Empire, to metallic sounds the dancers make with their swords and shields. There are still performances staged at festivals and other occasions today.

Chinese sword dance

The name that comes to mind first when talking about sword dance in China is certainly the "Banquet at Hongmen." This was an incident that occurred in the year 206 BC. In peace talks between Xiang Yu, the king of the Western Chu Dynasty, and Liu Bang, who later became the first emperor of the Former Han Dynasty, Xiang Yu's general Fan Zeng performed a sword dance during which he attempted to stab Liu Bang. Xiang Yu's uncle Xiang Bo read Fan Zeng's intention, and joined him in the dance, and thus prevented him from attacking Liu Bang. As a result, the plan to build a relationship of mutual trust ended in failure, which eventually led to the outbreak of the Chu-Han Contention, and after Xiang Yu's defeat, Liu Bang became the first emperor (Gaozu) of the Former Han Dynasty. This incident also became the subject of a piece of the Chinese traditional

ヨーロッパの剣舞

ヨーロッパで剣の舞というと、アラム・ハチャトゥリアンが一九四二年に作曲したバレエ音楽「ガイーヌ」の中の曲が浮かぶのではないでしょうか。これは、クルド民族が剣を持って舞う「レズギンカ」という民族舞踊をイメージしたものです。複数の男性が高く飛んだり空中で回転したりしながら剣を打ち合い踊ります。

また、スコットランドの民族舞踊の一つに、「ギリーカラム」と呼ばれる剣舞があります。これは、一五〇〇年代にスコットランドの部族長が、敵対していた他の部族を打ち負かした際、剣を地においてその上で踊った「勝利の踊り」が始まりです。現在は、地面に剣二本を十字に置き、その刃に触れないようにステップを踏む舞踊となっています。

performing art known as "Beijing Opera."

After the Han dynasty, swords were incorporated into court dance as power and status symbols, and such performances were at once a method of training positions, postures and patterns in martial arts.

European sword dance

When mentioning sword dance in Europe, many will probably think of the "Gayane" ballet with music composed by Aram Khachaturian in 1942. This music was inspired by a Kurdish folk dance called "Lezginka," which is performed with swords. The dance by multiple male performers involves big leaps and turns in the air, during which they clash their swords.

There also exists a folk dance incorporating swords in Scotland, called "Ghillie Callum." This was originally a "victory dance" performed by the heads of clans in Scotland in the 1500s after defeating rivaling clans. They used to dance above swords placed on the ground, and a form of Ghillie Callum is still performed today on pairs of crossed swords on the ground, while avoiding to touch the blades.

第二章

剣舞を
舞う
習う

Chapter

2

Training and
Performance of
Kenbu

剣舞を習ってみよう

第一章では、剣舞を「観る側」として、解説してきました。しかし、「観ているだけでは勿体無い！せっかくなら自分も舞台に立ってみたい」と思われた方は、ぜひ剣舞教室の門を叩いてみましょう。伝統芸能といろうと敷居が高いように思われますが、誰でも初歩から習い始めることができます。

教室の探し方

全国には一〇〇以上の流派があるといわれていますが、残念ながら看板を出していない・ウェブサイトがない・稽古は公民館を利用、というケースも多く、一般の人が探すことは少し困難です。

ウェブサイト検索以外の方法としては、①周囲（主に年配者）に詩吟をしている人がいたら、剣舞をしている人がいないか聞いてみる、②公民館で剣舞教室がないか聞いてみる、③近くのホール（文化会館など）で剣舞の発表会が行われていないか聞いてみる、というのが近道のように思います。発表会が行われていれば、終了後に出演者に声をかけることで、先生につなげてもらえるでしょう。公民館であれば、教室の日に訪れて、見学を申し込みましょう。

Training Kenbu

The introduction to kenbu in chapter 1 focused on the aspect of viewing, but I suppose that many readers will feel that they don't only want to watch performances, but try and do kenbu themselves. Even though traditional performing arts may sound like something with a rather high threshold, I would like to encourage you to just go and try, as schools offer lessons that teach everything you need to know from the very beginning.

How to find the right school

The number of kenbu schools in Japan is said to amount to over one hundred. Unfortunately, many of them are difficult to find because they have no catchy signboards, no website, or use local community centers for their lessons.

費用について

　一般的に、和のお稽古事は料金不明瞭、そして高い、と思われがちです。これはあながち間違っていません。実際に、日本舞踊（歌舞伎舞踊）は、かつて町人富裕層の婦人の習い事であったため、お月謝や発表会の御礼が高額な場合が多いです。しかしながら、質実剛健を旨とする武士の世界から生まれた剣舞は、日本舞踊と比べると費用が抑えられる傾向にあります。

　断定はできませんが、多くの教室は月一万円程度で始められるのではないかと思います。もちろん、流派によってさまざまなので、入門問い合わせ時に確認しましょう。

免許について

　日本の芸道ではほとんどが免許制度を採っています。これは、端的に言えば、流派の頂点たる宗家にどれくらい近づけたかを認定するものです。級位・段位の他、職種として師範代・師範を設けている流派が多いと思います。流派は一つの組織なので、長年所属するとそういった免許を取得することが勧められますし、取ってみると、なかなか気分の良いものです。

　しかし、たいていは上位の免状になるほど、免許料が高額になりますので、「何級（何段）までは取得必須か」、「師範取得に必要な費用」なども、気になる人は予め確認しましょう。

Fees

The charges for lessons in anything traditionally Japanese are generally considered to be somewhat unclear and rather high. This isn't entirely wrong. As Japanese dance (Nihon buyo) or Kabuki dance are things that mainly the wives of wealthy merchants used to study, monthly fees and performance charges are often very high. However, compared to Japanese dance for example, costs involved in kenbu as something that emerged from the samurai world of simplicity and sincerity tend to be relatively low. Although I cannot say this with certainty, I think that many schools offer training sessions starting at about 10,000 yen per month. There are of course also schools that treat kenbu on the same level as Japanese dance, so I recommend to inquire about fees first when contacting a school for available lessons.

Licensing

In the realm of Japanese performing arts, in most cases a licensing system is adopted. Plainly speaking, this is a way of certifying how close one gets to the status of the originator or head of the respective school. Next to instructors with a status or grade, there seem to be many schools that employ assistants and regular instructors. A school is an organization, and in order to stay with that organization for a long time, it is recommended to acquire such kind of license. Above that, it also feels nice to possess one.

お稽古に必要な道具

毎回のお稽古には刀や稽古着など、いくつかの道具を持参する必要があります。いずれも、お師匠さんから教えてもらえますので、指示されたものを購入して持参しましょう。

刀

剣舞は武道から発祥した舞台芸能ですので、もともとは真剣を使って舞っていました。今では真剣を使って舞う人は少なく、居合用の武道刀（模擬刀）を使います。重量は一キロ前後で、日本舞踊や殺陣で使う舞刀（ジュラルミン製）あるいは竹光とくらべると、ずっしりしています。女性や子どもなど力のない方は、舞刀を使う場合もあります。購入先やタイプ・長さは、お師匠さんに相談するのがベストです。

舞扇 (まいせん)

一般的に扇子というと、仰いで涼を得るための仰ぎ扇子が思い浮かびますが、舞台芸能では舞扇が使われます。能で使われる仕舞扇と同じ素材・構造ですが、一回り小さく、剣舞・詩舞の他にも日本舞踊や民謡舞踊にも使われます。

扇は和紙と竹で作られているため痛みやすく、お稽古用の安価な扇を都度買い替えていくことになります。舞台用（本番用）の扇子は、作品のテーマによって相応しい柄をお師匠さんと相談しながら用意します。

Training sessions and things to bring

Students are required to bring a number of items such as a sword and practice suit for each session. Your teacher will tell you exactly what you need, so just follow his or her instructions when purchasing the respective tools.

Swords

As kenbu is a performing art that developed from the realm of martial arts, it was originally practiced with a serious sword. Nowadays, only few performers dance with a serious sword, but most of them use an unsharpened sword for martial arts practice instead. A sword weights about one kilogram, and compared to the dance sword (made of duralumin) used in Japanese dance, or the bamboo sword used in tate (theatrical fighting scenes), it is quite heavy. Some women or children who don't have the physical power replace it with a dance sword. For the appropriate type, length, and place of purchase, I recommend to consult your kenbu master.

Dancer's fans

When talking about fans, you will probably think first and foremost of a device that gives you cool air in the summer, but there are also fans that are purely designed for use in performing arts. They are made from the same materials and in the same way as the shimai fan that is used in Noh, but are a bit smaller. Next to kenbu and shibu, such fans are also used in Japanese dance and folk dance.

A fan is made of Japanese paper and bamboo, and therefore breaks easily, so for training session you will keep buying cheep practice fans as necessary. For a performance – the real thing – your master will offer advice as to what kind of design will match the theme of your performance.

　着物や袴を着用して「舞う」のは、それなりに気を遣わなければならないものです。慣れていないと、思わぬところで引っかかったり、雑な所作になるため、日頃から着用しておく稽古をすることが大切です。

　着物は手首を隠れるくらいの袖の長さにしておくと、袖さばきを日頃から訓練できます。袴はお稽古では剣道袴がリーズナブルです。

足袋

裏地が綿のタイプを購入しましょう。ナイロンだと滑りが良すぎて舞には適しません。また、くるぶしで留めるための鞐（コハゼ）には五枚のものと四枚のものがあります。教室によっては五枚鞐が指定されている場合もありますので、お師匠さんに確認しましょう。

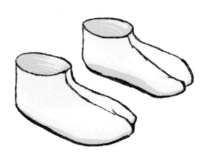

Practice suits (kimono and hakama)

"Dancing" wearing kimono or hakama requires a considerable amount of attention. When you are not used to wearing such items, you will find your costume getting caught somewhere, and your moves becoming sloppy, so getting used by wearing a kimono or hakama on a regular basis and in your lessons is essential.

Wearing kimono with sleeves that are long enough to cover the wrists can help you practice the handling of the sleeves on a daily basis. For hakama, kendo hakama are a reasonable choice to wear during your training session.

Tabi (socks)

I recommend getting tabi with cotton lining. Nylon socks tend to be too slippery, so those are not suited for dance. Furthermore, there are types with four and five clasps for fastening them around the ankles. Some schools specify that their pupils use those with five clasps, so you might want to confirm this with your master beforehand.

お稽古の流れ

　稽古の成果は舞台出演という形に結びつくことになります。しかし、すぐに舞台作品の振付に入るのではなく、型の稽古がはじめにあり、それから振付の稽古を行うのが通常です。一例として、筆者が所属する正賀流でのお稽古について説明します。

① 道場入り

道場に礼・お師匠さんにご挨拶、着替え。

② 刀礼

お稽古の前には、刀を使った座礼を行います。複数のお弟子さんと一緒にお稽古する場合は、入門順に並んで、お師匠さんと向い合せになります。座礼の作法には、武道式と舞踊式があり、流派によってどちらを採用しているかが異なります。（足をどちらから引くか等も異なります。）

③ 基本稽古（構え・運び・手の表情）

お稽古が始まったら、まずは舞の基本姿勢となる吊り腰、足運びの基本である摺足と武道歩き、さらに踏み出し（蹴り出し・板割り）、掛かり足といった脚さばきを練習します。さらに、手の表情の練習も行います。

Procedure of a training session

As kenbu is a form of performing arts, the results of its training are usually presented in the form of a stage performance. But your training won't address the choreography of a performance right away, as there is usually some formal training that has to be done first, and only after that, the focus of your practice will shift to choreography. As an example, let me explain the process in the case of training at the Seiga-ryu.

1) Entering the dojo

Upon entering the dojo (training hall), you bow and greet your master, before changing into your training suit.

2) Bowing with the sword

Prior to the start of your training session, you do a formal bow with your sword while seated. For sessions with multiple pupils, students line up in the order of entry to face their master. In terms of formal bows, there are two different styles – the martial arts style and the dance style – and it depends on the school which one is adopted for the training. (Differences include such details as how to pull your feet in.)

3) Basic practice (posture, movement, expression using hands)

The training usually begins with sessions teaching the basic "lowered waist" dance position, the basic, shuffling walking style and "martial arts walk," and other footwork such as keridashi and itawari. You will also practice expressive techniques using your hands.

姿勢・構え

舞台上では、客席との高さの違いを考慮し、「つり腰」と呼ばれるやや前傾の姿勢が基本となります。構えは「心の構え」ともいわれ、日本のどの芸道においても厳しく指導されます。「構え」の姿に、その人の、その道での、修行の凝結が表れるといえるでしょう。

つり腰

Tsurigoshi

つま先に少し重心をかけて前傾し、胸を張り、顎を引きます。この時、足は膝に少し緩みをもたせ、両肘は少し体からはなして張りましょう。目線は目の高さの遠くに。

The performer throws out his/her chest and pulls in the chin, and assumes a forward-leaning posture while gradually shifting the body weight to a position above the toes. The knees are slightly bent and rather relaxed, while the elbows are held away from the body. The performer gazes straight forward at eye level, and into the distance.

常の腰

Tsunenokoshi

特に意識しない、日常の腰。いわゆる「気をつけ」の姿勢です。

This usually unconscious posture is the so-called "ready position."

本構え

Hongamae

わし手持ちになり、脇の下は握りこぶし一つくらいあけ、肘をはります。

Hands are held in the washidemochi style, and elbows are spread out with both arms held about the width of a fist away from the body.

大名構え
Daimyogamae

本構えよりも広く脇を開き、両足は20-30cmぐらい離します。ひじは大きくはり、肩をやや上げましょう。

The arms are held further away from the body than in the hongamae, with elbows and shoulders higher and wider. The feet are about 20-30 centimeters apart.

座り構え
Suwarigamae

両膝を開き、つま先は立て、両手は足の付根に置きます。

Knees are opened, toes tightened, and both hands placed at the thighs.

箱足
Hakoashi

腰を充分に落とし、膝と足先は外に開きます。

The waist is significantly lower, and knees and feet are turned outward.

かかり足
Kakariashi

片方の足を斜め後ろに引きます。この時、姿勢が倒れないように注意します。また、前方の足が内足に入らないようにします。

The performer stands upright with one leg drawn back at a 45-degree angle, while carefully balancing the body and making sure that the other foot is not turned inward.

Posture and attitude

Considering the height difference between the audience and those on stage, kenbu is basically performed in a forward-leaning posture called tsurigoshi. "Attitude" also refers to the performer's mental attitude, which is subject to very strict instruction in any Japanese traditional art form. One may understand a performer's "attitude" as representing an aggregation of all of his/her previous training in the respective art.

スッ
スッ
スッ〜

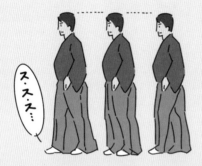

ス・ス・ス…

【運び足】

日本の舞の多くは、中腰姿勢ですり足を基調としています。すり足で舞台を移動する時は「歩く」とは言わずに「運ぶ」と言います。すり足は、足の裏があまり見えないように腰と腹に力を入れて、身体が上下しないように滑るように歩きます。すり足を上手に行うには、長年の訓練が必要です。

剣舞すり足（武道すり足）と舞すり足

Kenbu-suriashi (or Budo-suriashi) and Mai-suriashi

「武道すり足」は、武道的な強いタッチのすり足です。腰を比較的深く落とし、やや前方に体重を乗せながら、足を運びます。

「舞すり足」は、武道すり足よりも足幅を狭くし、膝は軽く緩める程度にして、姿勢は立てて運びます。いかにも舞らしい、柔らかい印象の運び方です。

Budo-suriashi is a firm, martial arts style of suriashi during which the waist is even lower than usual, and the body leaning even further forward.
For the mai-suriashi the feet stay closer together than in the budo-suriashi, and the overall posture is largely upright with the knees bent only slightly. The result is a very pliant, dance-like motion.

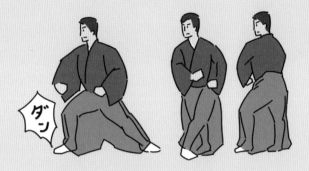

踏み出し（蹴り出し・板割り）
Keridashi (or Fumidashi/Itawari)

「踏み出し（蹴り出し・板割り）」は、剣舞の特徴の一つといって
も良いかもしれません。板を割ってしまうくらいに力強く足を踏
み出し、「バンッ」と音を立てます。演舞において力強さを表現す
るのに効果的に使われます。

Keridashi is one of the most characteristic movements in kenbu. The performer
stamps his/her feet so hard that they make a big noise and almost crack the
floorboards. This is an effective way to express power through dance.

Moving on stage (hakobi-ashi)

Many forms of Japanese-style dance are basically performed in a shuffling suriashi syle and a half-sitting posture. When
moving across the stage in the suriashi style, we speak of "hakobu" (lit. "to carry" or "to proceed") rather than "aruku"
(to walk). For the suriashi style, the performer strains the muscles around the waist and belly in order to proceed in a
sliding manner without moving the body up and down, and without showing much of the soles of his/her feet.
Mastering the suriashi style requires many years of training.

【手の表情】

演舞中の手の表情（形）によって、その瞬間を強く見せたいのか、柔らかく見せたいのか、随分と印象が違ってきます。また、片方の手が刀や扇で何かを表現していると き、反対の手が意識されずにダランとなっていることが、初心者の方にはよく見受けられます。舞のお稽古では、手足の指先まで意識をするようにしましょう。

こぶし
Kobushi

親指を中指の上に重ねて力強く握ります。肘の張り具合によって、全体の強弱の印象が変わります。

The performer makes a fist with the thumb tightly pressed against the top of the middle finger. The overall impression can be varied from weak to strong by changing the position/tension of the elbows.

わし手持ち
Washidemochi

ワシのくちばしに似ているところからこの名で呼ばれます。舞の基本とされる構えです。

This is one basic dance posture in which the hand is used in a way that makes it look like the beak of an eagle (washi).

割り手
Warite

親指だけ力を入れて離し、人差指から小指までをそろえます。

Four fingers of the hand are aligned, and only the thumb is firmly spread out.

はり手

Harite

手の指を一本一本、力を入れて離し、広げます。非常に強い印象を出したいときに使います。

The hand is opened, with each finger firmly spread out. This style is used for creating a very powerful impression.

男ざし

Otokozashi

指をしっかりにぎり、人差指で指します。

The hand is used to point at something with the index finger, while the other fingers are tightly gripped, as opposed to the loose grip of the so-called onnazashi style.

伏せ手と受け手

Fusete and Ukete

手のひらを下に向けた状態を伏せ手、手のひらを上に向けた状態を受け手と呼びます。

A hand held with the palm facing down is called fusete, and with the palm facing up it is called ukete.

Expressions of the hands

There are various patterns (kata) of using the hands in a dance performance to create very different instant impressions, ranging from great strength to softness and gentleness. When holding a sword or fan in one hand in order to express something, especially beginners tend to neglect the other hand, resulting in slovenly movements. One focus in the practice of kenbu is on how to use every finger and every toe consciously.

④扇子の稽古

刀だけでは表現しきれない様々な情景描写を、扇を使って表現します。作品のお稽古に入る前の基本練習として、扇の技法を覚えておくと、その後の見立てのお稽古（見立てについては第一章三十九〜四十四ページを参照）がスムーズになります。

【扇子の持ち方】

扇を装飾の道具として使う場合も、見立ての小道具として使う場合も、基本になるのはその持ち方です。帯からの取り出し方、納め方、握り持ち、平持ち（四指持ち）、つまみ持ち、親骨持ちなど、自由自在に扱えるようにお稽古しましょう。

握り持ち
Nigirimochi

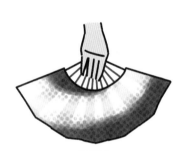

平持ち
Hiramochi

4) Practicing the use of a fan

For various scenes that cannot be properly described with a sword only, a fan is used as an additional tool. Mastering techniques of using the fan at the basic training stage before practicing the performance of concrete pieces will be helpful for getting the mitate (see page 38 in Chapter 1) right once you get to that stage later on.

Ways of holding a fan

There are several basic ways of holding a fan, whether it is used as a decorative element or as a tool for imitating certain actions. Through repeated training, performers develop a perfect command of the fan's usage in operations including pulling it out of the belt or tucking it away, or holding it in different ways using different (combinations of) fingers.

親骨持ち
Oyabonemochi

つまみ持ち
Tsumamimochi

くつろぎ持ち
Kutsurogimochi

地紙持ち
Jigamimochi

中骨持ち
Nakabonemochi

⑤刀法稽古

「刀法」という場合、二つの意味があります。一つは、刀の抜き差しや、斬り方のパターンなど、広く「刀の使い方」という意味で、「刀法の型」という言い方もします。初学者は、まず刀の基本的な扱い方を習います。

具体的には、刀の持ち方、帯び方、携え方、抜刀の仕方、納刀の仕方、安全面の配慮などです。

もう一つの意味は、「刀法一本目」「刀法二本目」のように、その流派で決められた一連の流れ（手順）をさします。

例えば、正賀流の「刀法一本目」は、一文字抜刀・正面斬り・胴斬り・唐竹割り・血振り・納刀、「二本目」は流し抜刀・袈裟斬り・両すくい斬り・血振り・納刀といった具合で、それぞれの「刀法の型」を組み合わせて構成されます。

この刀法の本数や名称、型の組み合わせは流派によって異なりますが、いずれも練習生が段階を踏んで稽古できるように構成されています。

なお、型の種類は武道（居合）と共通のものが多数ですが、舞台芸能の表現として独自に作られた型や、武道と同じ名称でも見せ方が異なる場合があります。

---

5) Practicing the use of a sword

"Using a sword" here has two different meanings. The first is the use of a sword in general, including kata (patterns) of sheathing, unsheathing or striking. Beginners first learn the basics of handling a sword, such as how to wear it, how to hold it, how to draw it and how to return it to the sheath, as well as aspects of safety.

The second meaning is the procedure (that differs depending on the school), or the order of "pattern one," "pattern two," etc.

"Pattern one" as taught at the Seiga-ryu, for example, is *ichimonji batto, shomengiri, dougiri, karatakewari, chiburi* and *sheathing;* "pattern two" is *nagashi batto, kesagiri, sukuigiri, chiburi* and *sheathing*. These are some of the different kata of which a performance is composed.

Numbers, names and combinations of kata vary from one school to the next, but all schools generally teach kata that trainees can practice step by step.

While there are many types of kata that kenbu shares with budo (iaido), there are others that were specifically created for expression in performing arts, or that have the same names but are performed differently from the kata in martial arts.

⑥ 作品稽古

基本練習が一通り済むと作品の振り付け稽古に入ります。まず詩文の内容や歴史背景を学び、次に振付を習いながら、振り付けの意味と解釈を学びます。スムーズに動けるようになったら、吟詠に合わせて舞う稽古をします。先生が適宜、形直しをしたり、間の取り方などを指導してくれます。気品を保ちつつ迫力を見せると同時に、丁寧な所作で細やかな詩心表現ができるよう、お稽古を重ねていきます。

⑦ 上がりの礼・掃除

お稽古が終わると、始めと同じように一列に並んで座礼をします。床拭きなどの掃除を行います。

6) Practicing choreography

Once you have completed the basic training as described above, you will start practicing the choreography of a performance. After studying the meanings and historical background of the poems used, you proceed to the choreography practice that includes also understanding the meaning of choreographic elements. Once your movements are smooth enough, you will start practicing dance to poetry recitation. Your master will correct your posture and teach you how to time movements and pauses among others. In the following sessions you will gradually learn to display forcefulness and gracefulness at the same time, and to express delicate sentiments through careful conduct.

7) Bowing and cleaning up

At the end of each training session, students line up as in the beginning, and bow while seated. After that they clean up, which includes wiping the floor.

Basic ways of using a sword (from unsheathing to sheathing)

1. 構え（携刀姿勢）

I. Holding the sword (kamae)

左手は親指を鍔にかけて、残りの四指で鯉口近くを握ります。

The thumb of the left hand is placed on the guard, while the other fingers grip the sheath near the mouth.

2.鯉口を切る

2. Loosening the sword (koikuchi o kiru)

静かに右手を下から柄にかけ、左手は上から親指を鍔にかけ、鍔を前に押しましょう。

As the right hand slowly grips the haft from below, the thumb of the left hand that holds the sheath from above pushes the guard away from the sheath.

3. 抜刀（抜きつけ）

3. Drawing the sword (nukitsuke)

刀を抜く動作が最初の一刀（攻撃）となる場合、これを抜き付けといいます。抜く速さは、徐・破・急が良いとされ、一刀必殺の鋭さをもたせます。このとき、左手は鯉口から離すことなく、小指を帯に押し付けて後方に引くようにしましょう。

When the sword is drawn for an itto (single stroke) attack, this is called nukitsuke. Regarding the speed of unsheathing, slow → medium → quick is considered to be an appropriate rhythm for achieving the poignancy that is necessary for killing the enemy with a single stroke of the sword. The left hand remains on the sheath near the mouth, whereas the little finger is pressed against the belt and pulls it back.

横から見たところ
Side View

4. 振りかぶり

4. Brandishing the sword (furikaburi)

切っ先を左耳にそって後ろを突くようなつもりで素早く刀を頭上に振りかぶります。この際、切っ先を水平より下げません。柄の握り方は、鍔下の縁金に右手の人差し指がかからないようにして握り、両手の間に指二本程度を空けます。小指と薬指を締め、他の指は緩めましょう。

The sword is quickly brandished over the head, moving the blade along the left ear so that the tip points to the back. The tip should not be lowered, as the motion should end with the sword in a horizontal position. There should be an interval of about two fingers between both hands. The little and the third finger are tightened, while the other fingers are relaxed.

5. 真向斬り（切り下ろし）

5. Vertical stroke (kirioroshi)

両脇を締めながら手の内をしめて、敵（「仮想敵」と言います。）の頭上付近から振り下ろす。まっすぐ振り下ろせていれば、太刀風というシュンという音がなります。（舞刀など軽い刀は鳴らないこともあります。）

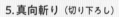

Both underarms are kept to the body, and the grip of the hands is tightened. The sword is thrusted down from a position above the head of the "hypothetical enemy." A straight vertical stroke will produce a swishing sound. (Some lighter dance swords don't produce any sound.)

6. 血振り

6. Shaking blood off the sword (chiburi)

相手を切った後、刀についた血を振り落とすことを「血振り」と言います。三通りの血振りがありますが、ここでは手首をかえして刀を右に開く血振りをしましょう。左手は次の納刀に備え、鞘を深く握ります。

After his/her stroke at the "enemy," the performer makes a so-called chiburi motion to shake off the blood from the sword. While there exist three different chiburi patterns, in this case the wrist is turned outward so that the blade of the sword faces to the right. Before sheathing the sword again, the left hand grips the sheath tightly.

7. 納刀

7. Sheathing the sword (noto)

血振りの後、左手鞘の鯉口をヘソ前に送ります。右肘と左肘を上手に動かして鯉口を棟にはわせ、切っ先を鯉口に納めるようにして、納刀します。

After shaking off the blood, the sheath is brought forward with the left hand until the mouth is near the navel. Make sure to move the elbows of both arms properly to insert the tip into the mouth of the sheath, and sheathe the sword smoothly.

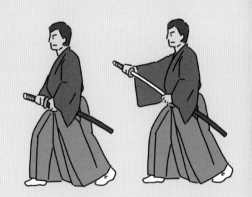

【抜刀中の構え】

刀の使術については、居合道や剣道（剣術）の型が元となっていますが、型によっては剣舞用に変化が加えられていたり、より見栄えを重視した独特の型があります。

晴眼（正眼）の構え
Seigan no kamae

横一文字の構え
Yoko-ichimonji no kamae

下段の構え
Gedan no kamae

Postures with the drawn sword

Regarding practice with the sword, movements are based on iaido and kendo (kenjutsu) patterns, whereas some patterns have been modified for use in kenbu. In addition, there are some original kenbu patterns with a stronger focus on visual aspects.

大八相の構え

Dai-hasso no kamae

八相の構え

Hasso no kamae

大上段の構え

Dai-jodan no kamae

上段の構え

Jodan no kamae

一文字くずしの構え
Ichimonji kuzushi no kamae

横構え
Yokogamae

縦一文字の構え
Tate-ichimonji no kamae

鍔返しの構え
Tsubagaeshi no kamae

脇構え
Wakigamae

流し構え
Nagashigamae

刃止めの構え
Hadome no kamae

Types of strokes: cutting motion (kiru)

袈裟斬り

Kesagiri

敵の肩口から斜めに切り下ろす斬り方です。切りおろした際、左こぶしはへそ前で止め、切っ先は水平よりわずかに下げます。

This is a diagonal stroke down from the enemy's shoulder. The stroke ends with the left hand on the haft stopping at the height of the navel, so that the sword points slightly downward.

逆袈裟斬り

Gyakugesagiri

正面の敵の脇腹から斜めに斬り上げる斬り方です。前足を踏み込むと同時に行うのがポイントとなります。

This is a diagonal stroke up from the enemy's side. For this pattern it is essential to make the stroke while simultaneously taking a step forward.

すくい斬り

Sukuigiri

逆袈裟斬りをアレンジした剣舞独特の型といえます。太刀筋（斬れるかどうか）を意識せずに、腕を回しながら刀を下から上にすくい上げます。

This original kenbu pattern can be understood as a modified version of the gyakugesagiri. Without caring about the effect of the stroke as such, the sword is thrusted upward with rotating arms.

胴斬り
Dogiri

敵の胴体を側面から打ちに行く
斬り方です。

This is a stroke aimed at the side of
the enemy's body.

回転払い斬り
Kaitenharaigiri

「胴斬り」と似ていますが、剣舞
らしく、よりダイナミックに腕
を回して、自身も回転しながら、
敵の胴体をを側面から打ちます。

Similar to the dogiri pattern, this stroke
aims at the enemy's side as well.
Typical for a kenbu pattern, however,
the rotating motion of the arms and
the entire body is much more dynamic.

唐竹割り（兜割り）
Karatakewari/Kabutowari

竹を真二つに割るように、腰を
充分に落として、上から刀を打
ち下ろします。これも、剣舞で
よく見られる刀技の一つです。

The waist is lowered, and the raised
sword is moved down in a vertical
cutting motion as if splitting a piece of
bamboo in two. This is another pattern
that is frequently seen in kenbu
performances.

刀で「斬る」以外に、「突く」があります。突きは、しっかりと腰を入れることが肝要です。

前方突き
Zenpozuki

後方突き
Kohozuki

Types of strokes: stabbing motion (tsuku)

In addition to cutting movements of the sword, there are also stabbing strokes. When performing stabbing strokes, it is important to take a solid stance.

両手突き
Ryotezuki

添え手突き
Soetezuki

舞台こそ剣舞の醍醐味！

お稽古をしばらく続けていると、ある時お師匠さんから舞台のお話をして頂けるでしょう。舞台の日が決まったら、本人はもちろんお師匠さんも、これまでにも増してお稽古に力が入るはずです。同時に、演舞のことだけでなく、衣装や小道具の準備、当日のアクセスなど、考えることがたくさんあります。一つずつ、お師匠さんや兄弟子さん・姉弟子さんに確認しながら、準備を進めましょう。

舞台当日は……

当日、会場に到着したら、まずはお師匠さんや会場でお世話になる方々に挨拶を行いましょう。続いて、舞台を確認しに行きます。客席から確認するしかない場合もありますが、催しによっては「場当たり」といって、開演前のわずかな時間に舞台を踏む機会が与えられる場合もあります。可能であれば、足袋を履いて舞台の滑り具合や、中央までの距離感を確認しましょう。

控室（楽屋）では、多くの方が着付けやお化粧をしています。互いに声掛けをしながら譲り合ってスペースを使いましょう。そしていよいよ出番直前。衣装の乱れがないか確認をし、息を整え、集中作業に入ります。集中する方法は人により様々ですが、軽く身体を動かしたり、頭の中でイメージをする人が多いと思います。

The real thing: performing kenbu

After a number of training sessions, at some point your master will start talking about staging a performance. Once the day of your performance is fixed, you will find yourself and your master increase your effort, and practice even harder than before. But at the same time, there are a number of things that also need to be considered, such as what piece to perform, what kind of costume to wear, what other items to use and how to organize them, and how to get to the venue of your performance. You will be preparing all these things one by one, while double-checking with your master and your senior fellow pupils.

The day of the performance

On the day of the performance, once you arrived at the venue, you should first greet your master and the people in charge at the venue. After that you will go and inspect the stage. It may happen that you are only able to inspect it from the audience seats, while in other cases there will be so-called "baatari" that allow you to stand on the stage for just a brief moment prior to the start of the performance. If possible, you may want to walk on the stage with your tabi in order to test how slippery it is, and also to get an idea of the distance to the center.

Backstage in the waiting or dressing room you will meet a lot of other people who get dressed and put on their makeup,

本番の緊張感は特別！

本番の演舞は、短ければ三分に満たないものであり、おそらくはあっという間に終わってしまった印象を持たれることでしょう。その中で、剣舞らしい一瞬の気合や最高の間合いを観客に観せるには、自らが作品に深く入り込めていることが何よりも重要となります。それには、呼吸のタイミングにまで及ぶ稽古を積んでいることが必要です。しかし、舞台

の緊張が共存する中で、稽古どおりの力を発揮するのは容易ではありません。それを如何に取りなし、作品としてまとめられる力をつけるには、ひとえに舞台経験を積んでいくしかないと思います。一回一回の舞台を大切にし、毎回反省をして、次はもっと良い演舞ができるように稽古をする……それが、「舞台人」としての理想的な姿です。

so you may have to arrange with everyone about the space you can use. Now it's only a few more minutes, and then it's your turn. After a final check to see if everything is alright with your costume, it's time to catch your breath and concentrate, for which different people seem to prefer different methods. Most people either keep moving their bodies lightly, or go through their performance in their minds.

That peculiar sense of tension

The actual performance will be less than three minutes long, so it will probably seem to you as if everything goes by in a flash. Whether you manage within that brief moment to show your audience some splendid moments of spiritedness and perfectly timed pauses largely depends on whether you managed to get deep into the material yourself. This you will only achieve if you have hours and hours of training under your belt that extends to such details as the timing of your breathing. But still it won't be easy to perfectly exert all the things you practiced with all the tension that will accompany you on stage. In my view, the only thing that will eventually help you get rid of this and develop the necessary skills to present a piece flawlessly is experience. Value every single performance, reflect on it afterwards, and return to your training with the eagerness to do it better next time… This is the ideal attitude of a "performer."

上達への道——「型」を稽古する意味とは?

「お稽古の流れ」で説明したように、たいていのお教室では型の稽古から入ると思います。型の稽古、振付の稽古、そして舞台出演という、一連のプロセスを踏むことが、剣舞という芸道への取り組み方の典型であり、これら全体を通して精神修養や礼儀作法を学ぶ場と捉えることが一般的です。

ところが、型稽古は単調で、それ自体がすごく楽しいという人は少ないでしょう。

実際、若い門下生にありがちなのが、型の稽古をせずに、作品の振付だけを学ぼうとするものです。あるいは、年配の門下生であっても、振付を覚えることが得意な人ほど、型の稽古を嫌がる傾向がみえます。

しかし、これらの人々は一様に良い舞手になることは少ないといえます。その一つの理由は、作品を覚える最中や、覚えた作品を舞として演舞する中では、意識が振付や詩吟音楽に向かってしまい、型に意識を向けるのが難しいということだと思います。また、振付は基本的に型の連続ですが、そのことが認識できていなければ、単なる「振り」として流してしまうことになるでしょう。

なぜでしょうか。それは、型が完成されることで、型に気を取られずに、型と型の移りや間、リズムなど、より高次の段階に早く進むことができるからです。

指導者側が型を重要と考えるのは、

108

Making progress: The importance of practicing kata

As outlined in "Procedure of a training session" above, I think most schools start their training with the practice of *kata*. Following the procedure of practicing *kata*, practicing choreography, and finally, doing a stage performance, represents a typical approach to the art of kenbu, and the common idea is that all this together presents an opportunity for exercising mental culture and etiquette.

The training of *kata*, however, is a very monotonous affair, and I suppose there aren't many people who consider such training to be great fun. As a matter of fact, young disciples often want to skip the pattern training as they want to move on to choreography right away. But also senior disciples tend to hate practicing *kata* especially when they are much better at memorizing choreographies.

However I think it is safe to say that most of these people will never be good performers. One reason for this is that, during the practice of a piece, or even during the performance of a dance piece that they have mastered, their attention will focus on the choreography, the poetry and the music, which makes it difficult to concentrate on the kata they need to perform. The choreography basically consists of a sequence of *kata*, and if a performer is not aware of this, he or she will just rattle through it as a chain of mere "gestures."

Now why is it that an instructor attaches so much importance to the *kata*? That's because a flawless delivery of *kata* will enable the performer to focus on other things such as the rhythm and the transition from one pattern to the next, and move on to an advanced stage without being preoccupied with the *kata*.

❖ 奈良期 *nara period*

和歌・剣太刀 [わか・つるぎたち]

Waka Tsurugi-tachi

大伴家持

Otomo no Yakamochi

剣太刀（つるぎたち）　いよよ研（と）ぐべし
古（いにしへ）ゆ　清（さや）く負（お）ひて　来（き）にし　その名（な）ぞ

歌人として有名な
大伴家持の、
武人としての心構えは？

作者の大伴家持（七一八〜七八五）は、奈良時代・大和政権に仕えた豪族で、大納言・大伴旅人の長男。いわゆる「武士」が誕生する以前の朝廷武官の家に生まれ、武人としてでもありました。大伴家持はこの和歌において、「武人の名門の名を曇らせることがないようにしなさい」と

にも多くの作品が収録され、三十六歌仙の一人とされています。（因みに新元号「令和」はこの万葉集が典拠とされています。その出典元は巻五、梅花歌三十二首序で「初春令月　気淑風和　梅披鏡前之粉　蘭薫珮後之香」です。）

さて、この時代において剣や太刀は、武器であるとともに、邪悪・穢れを祓い、清明さを回復させる神具でもありました。大伴家持はこの和歌において、「武人の名門の名を曇らせることがないようにしなさい」と

子孫への教訓を詠んでいます。振付例としては、堂々とした武人の趣で登場し、前半は刀剣の崇高さや大伴家持の凛々しさを、毅然とした動きで表現します。後半は、斬り付けや刀技で敵に対峙する姿勢を見せ、悠々と退場します。なおこの作品では、打刀を使用する場合であっても、太刀（佩刀）を意識した振付が要素に含まれることが多いです。

日本に現存する最古の歌集『万葉集』歌人としても広く活躍した人物です。

１１０

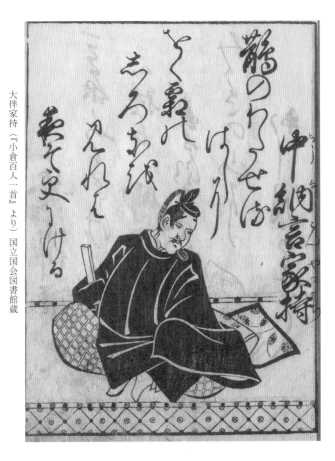

大伴家持　（『小倉百人一首』より）　国立国会図書館蔵

Tsurugitachi, iyoyo, togubeshi.
Inishieyu, sayakeku oite, kinishi, sononazo

Our swords we shall sharpen, now even more
The name we have cleanly assumed a long time ago

The author, Otomo no Yakamochi (718-785) was the eldest son of Otomo no Tabito, a powerful chief councilor of state who served the Yamato government in the Nara period. Born into the family of a military officer at the Imperial Court in times when the so-called "samurai" were yet to emerge, he was widely active both as a military man and as a poet. Otomo no Yakamochi is regarded as one of the "thirty-six major poets" of Japan, many of whose works are included in the Manyoshu, the oldest existing collection of classical Japanese poems. (A passage in the Manyoshu, by the way, is said to be where the recently introduced new era name "reiwa" originates from.)

At the time, swords were used as weapons and at once also as ritual tools for expelling evil and impurity, and thereby restoring purity. This poem, Otomo composed as a lesson to his descendants as to "how samurai are supposed to behave so that the names of their noble families are not obscured."

As a choreography example, the performer may enter the stage in the style of a stately samurai, and in the first half, express through resolute movements the sublimity of the sword and the gallantness of Otomo no Yakamochi. In the second half, we would then show some strokes and other skills with the sword while facing an (imaginary) enemy, before quietly walking off the stage. For the performance of this work, even when using a regular *katana*, choreographies often include elements that focus on the use of an older *tachi* (or *haito*) type of sword.

◆◆ 平安期 Heian era

和歌・吹く風を [わか・ふくかぜを]

Waka Fuku kaze wo

吹く風を　勿来の関と思へども　路も狭に散る　山桜かな

Minamoto no Yoshiie

源義家

「風よ、吹くなかれ」と歌った武将の心は？

作者の源義家（一〇三九〜一一〇六）は、平安中期の武将で、鎌倉幕府を開いた源頼朝の曾曾祖父にあたる人物です。石清水八幡宮で元服したことから「八幡太郎」、「八幡公」と呼ばれ、現在も毎年五月の端午の節句で男の子の成長を願って飾る武者人形として高い人気があります。この和歌は平安時代末期に編纂された

『千載和歌集』に収録されています。千載和歌集には優美典雅な趣の中にも無常観や静寂な境地が詠みこまれた作品が多く、本作品もその一つといえるでしょう。

義家は、前九年の役にて父・源頼義とともに戦い、後三年の役では陸奥守として参戦しました。詩文にある「勿来の関」というのは福島県にある関所で、「来るなかれ」（来てはいけない）という意味です。義家は、山桜が風に吹かれて花びらが美しく散

り舞う様子を、戦で多くの侍の命が散っていく様子と掛けて、「風よ、吹くなかれ」と詠んでいます。

振付例としては、前半は花びらが散る様を扇で美しく表現します。後半は戦の様子を斬り付けや刀技で表し、最後は赤い扇子で血しぶきを表すなどして、倒れた戦友の上にも花びらが舞い散る様子を演じます。

尾形月耕「源義家」（『義士四十七圖』より）国立国会図書館蔵

Fukukaze wo nakosonoseki to omoedomo, michimosenichiru yamazakurakana

No wind is supposed to blow in Nakonoseki, but now the scattered wild cherry blossoms leave only a narrow path

The author, Minamoto no Yoshiie (1039-1106) was a samurai in the mid-Heian period, and the great-grandfather of Minamoto no Yoritomo, who established the Kamakura Shogunate. In reference to his coming-of-age ceremony at the Iwashimizu Hachiman shrine, he is also known as "Hachiman Taro" or "Hachiman-ko," and the popular warrior doll that was modeled after him is still being put on display in Japanese homes every year on May 5 for the seasonal festival praying for the prosperity of male descendants. This poem is included in the Senzai wakashu poetry collection that was compiled at the end of the Heian period. It is one of several works in Senzai wakashu that, while generally displaying an elegant taste, contain tranquil meditations on the transient nature of life.

While serving in the Zenkunen War, Yoshiie, together with his father Yoriyoshi, at the time Governor of Mutsu Province and Commander-in-chief of the Defense of the North, fought Abe no Yoritoki and Sadato, and later served in the Gosannen War as the new Governor of Mutsu Province. Nakonoseki is the name of a checkpoint in Nakosomachi, Fukushima, whereas the meaning of "nakoso" is "not to be supposed to come." Yoshiie must have seen cherry blossoms scattered about by the wind as he passed the checkpoint. Regarding them as a symbol for the fleetingness of life, he compared the scattered blossoms to the soldiers who lost their lives in battle, and composed the poem addressing "the wind that is not supposed to come."

As a choreography example, the performer may use his fan to beautifully depict scattering petals in the first half, and in the second half, express war matters through sword strokes and other swordplay. At the end, he would use a red fan to express spraying blood, and finally, let once again blossoms flutter down onto the bodies of his fallen fellow soldiers.

❖ 平安期 Heian period

鉄拐峰に登る [てっかいほうにのぼる]

Tekkaiho ni noboru

梁田蛻巌
Yanada Zeigan

古塁烏啼いて　人を見ず

嶺雲澗水　共に春を傷ましむ

誰か知らん　夜半風前の笛

梅花を吹き落として　戦塵と作さんとは

一ノ谷の戦いに思いを馳せる

作者の梁田蛻巌（一六七二〜一七五七）は、江戸時代中期に明石藩藩主に仕えた儒学者です。源平争乱「一の谷の戦い」の旧跡である鉄拐山に登り、作詩したと思われます。このように江戸期の知識人が過去の出来事について詠んだものは多数残っており、剣舞演目にもよく登場します。

さて、平家物語に登場する「波際を敗走する平敦盛とそれを呼び止める熊谷直実」のエピソードは、合戦屏風図にも描かれるなど大変よく知られており、能や江若舞、文楽、歌舞伎など、他の芸能の演目にも取り上げられています。

本詩文に対する振付例としては、まず旅人（梁田）が鉄拐山に登り、古い陣屋の跡や鳥の鳴く声に寂しさを感じます。続いて源氏軍となり、馬で鉄拐山から逆落としに一の谷の平家軍を急襲する様を表します。後半では手負いの平敦盛となり、諦めの心境で得意の笛を手にします。そして波際を逃げようとしたところ、熊谷直実から呼び止められます。平敦盛は死の覚悟を以て熊谷の前に居直り、刀を地面に置き、胡座を組んで首を垂れるのです。最後は熊谷直実となり、自身の息子と同じ年齢くらいの平敦盛に手をかけるしかなかった自らの運命を嘆きつつ退場します。

114

Korui karasu naite hito wo mizu
Reiun kansui tomo ni haru wo itamashimu
Tareka shiran yahan fuzen no fue
Baika wo fukiotoshite senjinto nasantowa

Cries of ravens in an old camp, with no people in sight
The clouds on the mountains and the waters in the
valley remind us of past glories
I hear the sound of someone's flute at midnight
Only to find plum blossoms scattered across the
battlefield in the morning

The author, Yanada Zeigan (1672-1757), was a
Confucian scholar who served the lord of the Akashi
feudal clan in the mid-Edo period. This poem he
assumedly composed after climbing the Tekkai-san
mountain, a historic spot where the "Battle of
Ichinotani" took place during the Genpei War. There
exist a large number of poems like this one, in which
intellectual persons of the Edo period reflect on
occurrences of the past, and those are frequently
chosen as subjects for kenbu performances.

The famous episode in the Tale of the Heike, in which
Kumagai Naozane stops Taira no Atsumori in his
attempt to escape from the coast, is often depicted on
decorative folding screens, and has also become the
subject of various pieces in the realm of performing
arts, including Noh, Kowakamai dance, Bunraku and
Kabuki.

As an example of a possible choreography for a kenbu
performance, the performer may enter the stage as a
traveler (Yanada) who climbs the Tekkai-san mountain,
where the remains of an old camp and the cries of
ravens evoke in him a sense of loneliness. He would
then appear as a soldier of the Genji army, who rides
his horse back down from the mountain for an assault
upon the Heike army in Ichinotani. In the second half,
he would impersonate the wounded Taira no Atsumori,
who takes up his flute in a state of resignation. When he
tries to flee from the coast, he is held back by Naozane
Kumagai's words. Prepared to die, he returns until he
stands in front of Kumagai, puts his sword down, sits
cross-legged on the ground, and hangs his head. In the
final scene, he would then impersonate Naozane
Kumagai, who grieves over his fate having no choice
but to kill Atsumori even though he had realized that he
was only a boy about the same age as his own son.

一ノ谷合戦　国立国会図書館蔵

❖ **戦国期** Sengoku period

九月十三夜陣中の作
[くがつじゅうさんや　じんちゅうのさく]

Kugatsu Jusanya Jinchu No Saku

霜は軍営に満ちて　秋気清し　数行の過雁　月三更

越山併せ得たり　能州の景　遮莫　家郷の　遠征を思うを

上杉謙信　Uesugi Kenshin

越後の龍・謙信は陣中で月を見て何を思う？

作者・上杉謙信(一五三〇～一五七八)は、越後・春日山城(新潟県上越市)の山内上杉家十六代当主。屈指の戦上手とされ、後世に「越後の龍」と称されました。この漢詩は、天正五年(一五七七年)に能登畠山家の重臣・長続連率いる畠山軍と戦った「七尾城の戦い」にて、兵士の慰労を兼ねた月見の宴で詠んだものとされています。

振付例としては、戦を終えた謙信が、興奮冷めやらぬまま、陣地に戻って来ます(登場)。秋の夜のすがすがしい冷気の中、空を見上げると月光の下を雁が飛んでゆきます。そして激しい戦を回想して刀を振り、勝利によって手に入れた山々の景色を悠然と眺めます。ふと、故郷で我が身を心配する家族のことを思い出しますが、今は仕方ないのだと自らに言い聞かせ、次の戦地に赴くのです(退場)。

なお、謙信は生涯この一作しか漢詩を遺していません。それにも関わらず大変風雅な作品であることから、実は謙信自身の作品ではなく、ゴーストライターによるものだという説があります。

月百姿　霜満軍営秋気清数行過鴈月三更　謙信　国立国会図書館蔵

Shimo wa gun'ei ni michite, shuki kiyoshi
Suko no kagan, tsuki sanko
Etsuzan awase etari, Noshu no kei
Samoarabaare, kakyo no ensei wo omou wo

Military camps all over in the frost, in the fresh autumn air
geese fly by in front of the moon
Having conquered the mountains of Ecchu, now I look down upon Noto
Those back home will be worried about our expedition though

The author, Uesugi Kenshin (1530-1578), was the 16th head of the Yamanouchi-Uesugi family at Kasugayama Castle in Echigo (Joetsu, Niigata). Known for his outstanding skills in battle, he was posthumously nicknamed "Dragon of Echigo." He is said to have composed this poem during a moonlight banquet honoring the services of the soldiers who defeated the Hatakeyama forces lead by Cho Tsugutsura, the chief vassal of the Noto Hatakeyamas, in the "Battle of Nanao-jo Castle" in 1577.

As a choreography example, the performer may appear as Kenshin who, while still excited after the battle, returns to his position. In the refreshing chill of the autumn night, he looks up to the sky, and sees wild geese flying in the moonlight. Recollecting the fierce battle, and while brandishing his sword, he calmly looks across the mountains that he made his own through his victory. For a brief moment he thinks of his relatives who must be worrying about themselves in his hometown, but then he tells himself that there is nothing he can do about that now, and leaves (the stage) for the next battle front.

This is the only Chinese-style poem that Kenshin wrote in his lifetime, however its style is so elegant that some assume that it was in fact composed by a ghost-writer rather than by Kenshin himself.

❖ 戦国期 Sengoku period

偶作 [ぐうさく]

Gusaku

武田信玄 Takeda Shingen

鏖殺す　江南十萬の兵　腰間の一劍　血猶お腥し

竪僧は識らず　山川の主　我に向って　慇懃に姓名を問う

僧に名を問われた　意味は…

作者の武田信玄（一五二一～一五七三）は、甲斐武田家十九代当主。天文二十二年（一五五三年）から永禄七年（一五六四年）まで、上杉謙信と五回にわたり川中島で戦ったことで有名な戦国時代の武将です。信玄は「人は石垣、人は城、人は堀、情けは味方、讐（あだ）は敵なり」という言葉を残しています。信頼のできる人は城に匹

敵するという意味です。

この漢詩は信玄が30歳代の頃に詠んだものと言われています。

ある日、ひとりの僧侶が自分の名を尋ねてきました。数々の戦功を挙げ、このあたりの山川まで治める自分に対して名を尋ねてきたことに、信玄は腹を立ててしまいます。しかし、よくよく考えてみると、僧侶はそんな信玄を諫めようと、敢えて名前を聞いたのかもしれません。信玄は、このエピソードを漢詩に残すこ

とで、自戒しようとしたのです。

振付例としては、前半で若く血気溢れる信玄の勇猛ぶりを刀で大いに表現します。途中、僧侶に人代わりし、そんな信玄に名を尋ね、信玄の怒りに触れる様子を演じます。最後は、再び人代わりして信玄となった演者が、僧侶の諭しに気づき反省する様子を演じます。

武田上杉川中嶋大合戦の図　国立国会図書館蔵

Osatsusu, konan juman no hei
Yoken no ikken chi nao namagusashi
Juso wa shirazu sansen no nushi
Ware ni mukatte ingin ni seimei wo tou

I who have killed hundreds of thousands in the south
With a sword at my side that is still blood-smeared
Am the ruler of this region, but that never occurred
To the boy priest as he gallantly asks my name

The author, Takeda Shingen (1521-1573), was the 19th head of the Kai-Takeda clan. He was also a famous military commander in the Sengoku period, who faced Uesugi Kenshin in a total of five battles at Kawanakajima between 1553 and 1564. One of his most famous quotes literally translates into "A man is a castle a man is a stone wall a man is a trench. Mercy is a friend resentment is an enemy," meaning that a reliable person is equal to a castle.

Takeda is said to have composed this poem when he was in his thirties, after being asked his name by a priest. A man who had achieved many distinguished feats, and who had been ruling every mountain and every river in the region, Takeda got angry about the fact that he was asked for his name. But when thinking about it, the priest's inquiry was perhaps meant as a warning, and Takeda probably made this episode into a poem in order to admonish himself.

As a choreography example, in the first half the performer may use his sword to graphically express the young and overly vigorous Shingen's boldness. He would then transform into the priest, who asks Shingen for his name and thereby aroused his anger. In the final scene, he would impersonate Shingen once again, who reflects on himself after recognizing the priest's intention.

❖ 江戸期 Edo period

四十七士 [しじゅうしちし]

Shijushichishi

臥薪嘗胆 幾辛酸

一夜 剣光 雪に映じて寒し

四十七碑 猶ほ主を護る

凛然冷殺す 奸臣の肝

大塩平八郎 Oshio Heihachiro

江戸中期に世間を賑わせた大事件「赤穂事件」を題材にした作品

作者の大塩平八郎は、江戸時代後期の武士で儒学者。この漢詩は、歌舞伎や文楽などの題材としても人気の高い「赤穂浪士」について詠んだものです。

元禄十四年（一七〇一）三月十

四日、播磨赤穂藩（兵庫県赤穂市周辺）三代藩主の浅野内匠頭長矩が、高家・吉良上野介義央の仕打ちに恨みをつのらせて、江戸城「松の大廊下」で彼に斬りつけました。浅野内匠頭は即日切腹を命じられましたが、家来である赤穂藩の浪士たちは、これが「喧嘩両成敗」の原則に反するとして、吉良上野介も処罰を受けるべきと主張します。が、認められず、元禄十五年（一七〇

四十七士（『大日本歴史錦繪』より）国立国会図書館蔵

Gashinshotan ikushinsan
Ichiya kenko, yuki ni eijite samushi
Shijushichi hi, nao shu wo mamoru
Rinzen reisatsusu, kanshin no kan

Sleeping on the firewood, these were days of hardship and pain
The night was freezing cold, the glittering swords reflected in the snow
The tombstones of the forty-seven are protecting their lord still today
Dignified and cold-hearted, they killed the deceitful Shogunate retainer's guts

The author, Oshio Heihachiro, was a samurai and Confucian scholar in the late Edo period. This poem is about the forty-seven ronin, whose story is also a popular subject of Kabuki and Bunraku pieces.

On March 14, 1701, Asano(Takumi no Kami) Naganori, the third-generation lord of the Harima Ako faudal clan (around the city of Ako in Hyogo), slashed Kira (Kozuke no Suke) Yoshinaka with a sword at Edo Castle, prompted by his increasing grudge regarding the man's conduct. Asano was ordered to commit seppuku on the same day, but his vassals, the ronin of the Ako feudal clan, regarded this as being against the "Kenka Ryoseibai" principle, and claimed that Kira should be punished as well. When their claims were rejected, in the night of December 14, 1702, the forty-seven Ako ronin under Oishi Kuranosuke invaded Kira's house. After the incident, all of them committed seppuku, and like their lord, were buried at the Sengaku-ji Temple in Tokyo.

As a choreography example, in the first half the performer may depict the scenery of the Ako ronin's invasion into Kira's house on a signal from Oishi Kuranosuke. In the second half, he would finally discover the targeted prince Kira, cut his head off, make a deep bow in the direction of the Sengaku-ji where his lord is buried, and report the revenge.

二、十二月十四日深夜、大石内蔵助率いる四十七名の赤穂浪士が、吉良上野介邸に討ち入りました。事件後、彼らは切腹に処され、主君と同じく東京の泉岳寺に葬られています。

振付例としては、前半に大石内蔵助の合図で吉良邸に討ち入る赤穂浪士たちを演じます。後半は標的の吉良公を見つけて遂に首を落とし、主君が眠る泉岳寺の方向に向かって深々と礼をし、主君の無念を晴らしたことを報告します。

❖ **幕末期** End of the Edo period

和歌・鉾とりて [わか・ほことりて]

Waka Hokotorite

鉾とりて月見るごとにおもふ哉
あすはかばねの上に照かと

土方歳三 Hijikata Toshizo

戦いの中で
最期を覚悟した一首

作者の土方歳三(一八三五〜一八六九)
は一八六三年、新選組を結成し、「鬼
の副長」として、近藤勇や沖田総司
らとともに京都市中の治安維持に当
たり、倒幕論者らを取締まりました。
鳥羽伏見の戦いに敗れた後も新政府
軍に抵抗し、北海道の箱館五稜郭の
戦いで指揮をとり、最後は銃弾に倒
れました。

新選組は明治・大正期には賊軍と
されていましたが、昭和期から評価
が見直され、昭和四〇年代に小説や
ドラマを通じて、新選組ブームが起
こりました。彼が使っていた刀のう
ち、「和泉守兼定」「大和守源秀國」
「葵紋越前康継」の三振りは、現在も
博物館などで見ることができます。

この和歌は、二〇一一年に京都の
霊山歴史館で見つかったもので、土
方歳三の辞世の句だと考えられてい
ます。「鉾を手にし、月をみるごとに

思うのだ。明日は自分の屍に月の光
が照るのかもしれないと。」

振付例としては、前半は殺伐とし
た剣技で市中を取り締まる様子を表
し、刀剣に己の人生と身命を託した
気持ちを表現します。後半は防戦的
に戦って潔く散りゆく様子を見せる
か、もしくはその直前の死地に向か
うまでを演じます。

五稜郭　函館市教育委員会提供

Hokotorite, tsukimiru goto ni omou kana
Asu wa kabane no ue ni teru ka to

Every time I take my halberd and look up to the moon
I imagine that it might shine on my corpse tomorrow.

The author, Hijikata Toshizo (1835-1869), established the Shinsengumi in 1863. As vice commander, alongside the likes of Kondo Isami and Okita Soji, he was responsible for the maintenance of peace and order in Kyoto, clamping down on those involved in the anti-Shogunate movement among others. Even after losing the Battle of Toba-Fushimi, he continued to resist the new government, and after leading the Battle of Goryokaku in Hakodate, Hokkaido, he was finally killed by a bullet.

While the Shinsengumi was considered as a rebel army in the Meiji and Taisho eras, the association has been reevaluated since the early Showa period, resulting in a Shinsengumi boom in novels and plays of the late 1960s and early '70s. From among the swords that Hijikata used, "Izumi no Kami Kenesada," "Yamato no Kami Minamoto no Hidekuni" and "Echizen Yasutsugu" are still on display at museums today.

This poem was discovered in 2011 at the Ryozen Museum in Kyoto, and is regarded as Hijikata Toshizo's death poem.

As a choreography example, in the first half the performer may express the way Hijikata controlled the city with his fierce swordsmanship, and illustrate the mindset of entrusting his life and body to the sword. In the second half, he may either depict how Hijkata manfully dies while continuing his defensive fight, or the time just prior to that, with Hijikata on his way into death.

❖ 情景詩 Landscape poetry

Fujisan

富士山 [ふじさん]

石川丈山 Ishikawa Jozan

仙客来り遊ぶ　雲外の巓　神龍栖み老ゆ　洞中の淵

雪は紈素の如く　煙は柄の如し　白扇倒に懸かる　東海の天

神龍住まう霊山を扇で舞う

世界文化遺産「富士山」は、静岡県と山梨県に跨る標高約三七七六メートルの独立峰で、日本随一の美景と神秘を誇る霊山として、古来より多くの人がこの山を詩歌にしたためてきました。江戸初期の武士で代表的漢詩人である石川丈山（一五八三〜一六七三）もその一人です。現在は休火山である富士山ですが、この詩が読まれた当時は、噴煙を上げる活火山でした。詩意は、「仙人が来て遊ぶといわれる神聖な富士山の頂きは、雲を突き抜けて高くそびえている。山頂にある洞窟の中の淵には、神龍が年久しく栖んでいると伝えられている。山頂あたりは純白の雪に覆われ、ちょうど白絹（しらぎぬ）を張ったようで、立ち昇る噴煙は、その扇の柄のように見える。まるで東海の大空に白扇が逆さまにかかっているようだ。」というものです。

本作は、扇のみで舞う詩舞として扱うことが多く、複数名の群舞としてリサイタル等でもよく舞われています。漢詩で表現された内容を具象化したり、抽象的表現で富士山の大いなる美しさとその付近の景観を表現します。なお、彼の晩年の住居は「詩仙堂」と名付けられ、今も京都に保存されています。

富士山

Senkaku kitari asobu, ungai no itadaki
Shinryu sumi oyu, dochu no fuchi
Yuki wa ganso no gotoku, kemuri wa e no gotoshi
Hakusen sakashima ni kakaru, tokai no ten

The peak of the sacred Mt. Fuji, where the hermits gather, rises high above the clouds
In the water in the cave, the divine dragon has been living for a long time they say
The peak is covered with pure white snow like silk, and the rising smoke spreads like a fan
It looks as if a white fan was hanging upside down in the sky above Tokai

At ca. 3,776 meters above sea level between Shizuoka and Yamanashi, the World Heritage Site of Mount Fuji (Fujisan) prides itself for being a mysterious sacred mountain that is at once one of the most beautiful sights in Japan. Since ancient times, it has inspired countless people to write poems about it, including also Ishikawa Jozan (1583-1673), a samurai and representative poet of the early Edo period. Presently a dormant volcano, at the time this poem was written, Mt. Fuji was still a smoking, active volcano.

When recited in the form of dance, this poem is frequently performed with a fan only, often also as a group dance by multiple performers, either by embodying the poem's contents, or by rather abstract gestures that communicate the magnificent beauty of Mt. Fuji and the surrounding landscape. The place where Ishikawa spent his last days came to be known as Shisen-do Temple, which is preserved to this day in Kyoto.

中国の漢詩

これまで、主に武士や出家僧が詠んだ漢詩、すなわち日本漢詩を取り上げてきましたが、漢詩といえば本場は中国です。漢詩は、紀元前八〇〇年以前に誕生し、最古の漢詩集は、儒教の「四書五経」のひとつ、「詩経」であるといわれています。紀元後六一八年の唐王朝には、李白や杜甫らが登場し、それまでの句数（行数）を定めない「古詩」から、八句からなる「律詩」や、四句からなる「絶句」などの形が定まり、以降の時代の漢詩へと受け継がれてゆくこととなります。

剣舞の作品も、多くは、この絶句や律詩を扱います。吟士や詩舞の舞手などの中には、日本漢詩よりも中国漢詩により親しみを持っている方も沢山います。

俗を考慮するならば、日本の着物と袴ではなく、漢服を着用し、中国刀を使用することになるでしょう。一方で、日本が漢詩などの漢文化を長年に渡って受容し、侍（日本人）として漢詩に向き合うという考え方をとるのであれば、衣装は武士の装束である着物と袴、刀は日本刀で差し支えありません。その時々の舞台の演出としてどちらの考え方を取るか選択すれば良いというのが、一般的な捉え方です。

中国漢詩をどのように舞うか？

ところで、剣舞・詩舞で中国漢詩を舞う場合は、装束や持ち道具をどうするかの検討が必要になります。もし、詩の作者や詠まれた時代の風

Chinese poetry

Up to this point I have mainly talked about Chinese poetry composed by samurai or Buddhist priests – in other words, Chinese-style poems written by Japanese. As a matter of course, Chinese poetry originated in China, before 800 BC. The oldest known collection of Chinese poems is said to be Shikyo (The Book of Songs), one of the "Nine Chinese Classics of Confucianism." Appearing in works from the Tang dynasty (618-907) were the likes of Li Bai (Li Po) and Du Fu, at a time when Chinese poetry underwent a transformation from the old style with unspecified numbers of verses/lines, to such formally fixed styles as risshi (8 verses) and the so-called Chinese quatrain, which defined the type of Chinese poetry that was eventually handed down through the generations.

Many kenbu pieces are based on these quatrains and risshi, and a lot of reciters and shibu performers are in fact more familiar with native Chinese poetry than with Chinese-style poems composed by Japanese.

How to dance to Chinese poetry

For performances of kenbu or shibu based on Chinese-style poems, performers need to think about what kinds of costumes and tools they want to use. Those who take into consideration the authors of the respective poems, and the manners and customs at the time of their creation, choose Chinese clothes rather than Japanese kimono and hakama, and use Chinese swords. On the other hand, Japan has been incorporating Chinese poetry and other forms of Chinese culture for centuries, and when we consider that it is a matter of (Japanese) samurai engaging in Chinese poetry, they may as well choose the samurai attire of kimono and hakama, and Japanese swords. The general consensus is that performers should choose either approach depending on the material and choreogrpahy of the piece they are going to show.

涼州詞　　王翰 作

葡萄の美酒　夜光の杯

飲まんと欲すれば　琵琶

馬上に催す

酔うて　沙場に臥す　君

笑うこと莫かれ

古来　征戦　幾人か回る

八陣の図　　杜甫 作

功は蓋う　三分の国

名は成る　八陣の図

江　流るるも　石　転ぜず

遺恨なり　呉を　呑むを　失す

従軍行　　王昌齢 作

秦時の明月　漢時の関

万里　長征して　人　未だ還らず

但　竜城の飛将をして　在らしめば

胡馬をして　陰山を　渡らしめず

楓橋夜泊　　張継 作

月落ち　烏啼いて　霜　天に満つ

江楓　漁火　愁眠に対す

姑蘇城外の　寒山寺

夜半の鐘声　客船に到る

峨眉山月の歌　　李白 作

峨眉山月　半輪の秋

影は　平羌江水に入って流る

夜　清渓を発して　三峡に向う

君を思えども見えず　渝州に下る

江南の春　　杜牧 作

千里　鶯　啼いて　緑　紅に映ず

水村山郭　酒旗の風

南朝　四百八十寺

多少の楼台　煙雨の中

剣舞を
深める
広げる

Chapter

3

Deeper and Wider

剣舞の歴史

第一章で剣舞の成り立ちを大まかに説明しましたが、ここで
はもう少し詳しく述べることにしましょう。実は、剣舞の歴史
といっても、撃剣興行以前の史料が残っているわけではなく、現
在手に入る資料の多くは、明治中期以降に書かれた、各流派で
独自にまとめられたテキスト類となっています。

その中でも剣舞の歴史が最も体系的にまとめられた書籍は、吟
詠家・大野正一氏が昭和五一年に発行した『剣舞の歴史』です。
前半の四十二頁が剣舞の歴史、次の十五頁が他の舞台芸能や武
道との関係および振付や表現に関する芸道論、最後の一一八頁
が、当時活動していた全国の八十八流派の系統図となっていま
す。本章の執筆にあたり参考にさせていただきました。

撃剣興行

それでは、改めて剣舞の歴史を撃剣興行から振り返ってみま
しょう。

舞台芸能としての剣舞が撃剣興行からスタートしたことは第

In this chapter I will dig "deeper" into the matter by discussing the history of kenbu, along with its contemporary significance and its accomplishments. I will also offer views from a "wider" perspective on outreach ativities, through an introduction of my own Samurai Kenbu Theater as well as interviews with the heads of kenbu schools throughout Japan.

I would like to encourage you, the reader, to join me in the discussion of the spirit of kenbu and ways of grasping it.

1. The History of Kenbu

Following the rough overview of the history of kenbu in Chapter 1, now let me take a closer and more detailed look. As a matter of fact, there are no historical documents that illustrate the situation prior to the emergence of fencing performances, and most of the materials that are available today are texts that were individually put together by the different schools around the middle of the Meiji period or later.

Among them, Kenbu no rekishi ("The history of kenbu"), published by gin'ei performer Ono Shoichi in 1976, is the one book that offers the most systematic overview of the history of kenbu. The first 42 pages are dedicated to the history of kenbu, followed by 15 pages illustrating the relationships between kenbu and other forms of performing and martialarts, as well as accomplishments in terms of choreography and style. The last 118 pages provide a system diagram including all 88 nationwide schools that existed at the time, which I used as a reference for the writing of this chapter.

一章で紹介しました。撃剣興行が当時衰退の一途を辿っていた剣術の技術継承に一役買い、また剣舞の舞台芸能としてのスタートになった点で、その歴史上の意義は非常に大きいといえます。撃剣興行がなぜ成功を収めたのか、そこには二つの理由があると考えられます。

①多くの撃剣家が撃剣興行に参加した大きな理由の一つに、かつての武士階級（士族）の経済的困窮があります。廃刀令と秩禄処分によって、元武士は代々先祖から引き継ぐはずだった家禄がなくなり、自ら商売をするか、勤めに出ないことには、日々の生活の糧が得られない状況に陥りました。しかしながら、商売などしたことのない元武士が、代々商売をしてきた町人衆と戦ってビジネスチャンスをモノにすることは、非常に難しいことだったに違いありません。榊原鍵吉が撃剣興行を主宰したのには、こうした元武士たちの経済的支援が大きく意識されていました。

②もう一つは、市民の剣術・武芸への憧れが挙げられます。撃剣興行はまたたく間に全国に広がりましたが、当然ながら観客がいなければ成立はしません。江戸時代には、剣術道場に一般市民が立ち入って観る機会はなく、一種の憧れの対象でもありました。撃剣興行は、一流の剣術家たちが試合をする様子を観られるとあって、市民の大ブームになったのです。その合間に

Fencing performances

Let me first take another look at the history of kenbu from the trend of fencing performances.

I mentioned in Chapter 1 that kenbu as a performing art has its origins in show fencing performances. When considering the role that fencing performances played in the technical succession of swordsmanship that continued to decline at the time, along with the fact that they marked the start of kenbu as a performing art, one understands their great historical significance. There are two possible reasons for the success that fencing performances achieved.

One major reason why many swordsmen engaged in show fencing was the economic poverty of the former samurai class. Through the law banning the private possession of swords, and the abolition of hereditary stipend, former samurai lost the hereditary stipend they were supposed to take over from their ancestors, which put them in a situation where either starting their own businesses or getting employed were the only ways of earning their daily bread. However, for former samurai who had no experience doing business whatsoever, competing with the local merchants that had existed for generations surely was a forlorn undertaking. In this respect, the fencing performances that Sakakibara Kenkichi began to organize attracted their attention as a possible source of economical support for former samurai.

The second reason is related to the citizens' general admiration toward swordsmanship and military arts. Show fencing spread across the nation in a wink, and as a matter of course, such performances only work when there is an audience. In the Edo period, there were no opportunities for general citizens to enter a fencing dojo and watch a fencing match,

創流期

撃剣興行は、風紀上の問題や、撃剣家が警察や軍に入っていくようになったことが理由で、数年の間に衰退してしまいます。

それでも、詩吟に合わせて刀で舞うという芸能様式が多くの人の目に触れたことは間違いありません。明治十年代に盛り上がった自由民権運動の集会では、聴衆を集めるための前座として用いられるなどしました。また、明治十七年には神田の錦輝館で詩吟と剣舞の会が開かれました。

そして同時期より、撃剣興行に携わっていた薩摩国出身の日比野正吉（雷風）が本格的に剣舞の研究を始めます。東京帝国大学の文学博士、重野安繹の助言を受け、居合術を基本としながらも、空手や能、日本舞踊など他の武道・芸術的要素を加えた剣舞を研究し、明治二十三年に神刀流を創流しました。撃剣興行で行われていた「剣舞」は、自ら吟を詠いながら、それぞれが思うままに刀を振っているだけのものであったのに対し、日比野雷風は吟士を別に立てて吟者と演者を分け、また詩の内容に合った振り付けを施してそれを統一のものとして門下に指導をしました。

so fencing was for them an object of admiration of sorts. As fencing performances were events at which people were able to witness fencing matches between leading swordsmen, they enjoyed immense popularity among citizens. The same goes also for kenbu performances that were shown in between.

The establishment of schools

Due to issues related to public morals, and the fact that swordsmen began to join the police or the army, show fencing declined over the course of a few years. However it is certain that there were still opportunities for many people to enjoy the performing arts format of poetry recitation combined with dance using swords. At meetings of the democratic popular rights movement that flourished around 1880, such performances were used as opening attractions in order to draw audiences, and in 1884, an event with shigin and kenbu was held at the Kinkikan in Kanda.

Around the same time, Hibino "Raifu" Masayoshi, a man from Satsuma who had been involved in show fencing, began to engage in serious studies of kenbu. On the advice of Shigeno Yasutsugu, doctor of literature at Teikoku University in Tokyo, he studied kenbu as a performing art that incporporated elements from other forms of martial or performing arts such as karate, noh and Japanese dance on a foundation of iaido techniques of drawing a sword, before finally establishing the Shinto-ryu in 1890. As opposed to the "kenbu" that was included in fencing shows – basically performers just brandishing their swords as they pleased while chanting Chinese poetry – Raifu Hibino separated the dance and poetry parts by introducing a dedicated reciter, worked out original choreographies in tune with the poems' contents, and went on to teach this integral format to his pupils.

神刀流の他にも、明治二十三年〜二十八年、源流となる剣舞流派が各地で誕生しました。下記はその主な流派です。これらの他にも、江戸期から続く剣術・居合道場が剣舞の指導を始めたケースもあります。

- 土佐派弥生流…秦霊華（長宗我部林馬）が刀流を基調に創流。
- 至心流…宮入清正が創流
- 金房流…金房冠一郎が歌舞伎を基調に創流
- 敷島流…佐野星山が、剣術　居合術を基調に創流
- 菊水流…藤田南海が創流
- 紫山流…北川是治が創流
- 立花流…小林義雄が創流
- 白刃流…日下部秀行が創流

日清戦争・日露戦争

神刀流創始者の日比野雷風をはじめ、各流派の指導者たちは精力的に勢力拡大に努め、それは次第に、軍国主義に傾倒する国家体制に接近する形となっていきます。日比野自身、東郷平八郎をはじめ多くの軍人や、強硬な国権論を主張した國民新聞

In addition to the Shinto-ryu, a number of schools that represent the origins of kenbu emerged across Japan between 1890 and 1895. Below is a list of the most important schools. Next to these, there are also fencing and iaido schools that have existed since the Edo period, and that later started offering also kenbu training.

- Tosa-ha Yayoi-ryu: founded by Hata Reika (Chosokabe Rinma) based on the Shinto-ryu
- Shishin-ryu: founded by Miyairi Kiyomasa
- Kinbusa-ryu: founded by Kanabusa Kanichiro based on kabuki
- Shikishima-ryu: founded by Sano Seizen based on techniques of fencing and drawing the sword
- Kikusui-ryu: founded by Fujita Nankai
- Shizan-ryu: founded by Kitagawa Yoshiharu
- Tachibana-ryu: founded by Kobayashi Yoshio
- Hakujin-ryu: founded by Kusakabe Hideyuki

The Sino-Japanese War and the Russo-Japanese War

Raifu Hibino, the founder of the Shinto-ryu, and other instructors from the respective schools energetically worked to expand the sphere of their influence, while gradually moving closer to the political system that was devoted to militarism at the time. Many soldiers, including Togo Heihachiro and also Hibino himself, operated with support from Tokutomi Soho, a writer for the Kokumin Shimbun newspaper and unyielding adcovate of the theory of national

の記者・徳富蘇峰の賛助を得ながら活動していました。日清戦争（明治二十七年）と日露戦争（明治三十七年）という二つの対外戦争においては、入隊の壮行会や陣営の激励、戦勝祝いの場など、あちこちで剣舞が舞われました。

そのため、剣舞が発祥した明治初期は、戦国時代の武将の戦いぶりを詠んだ『不識庵機山を撃つの図に題す』や、江戸中期の赤穂事件を題材にした『四十七士』など、近代以前の武士の姿が演じられることが多かったのですが、国権論が盛り上がってからは、それを直接的・間接的に詠み込んだ漢詩文が取り上げられたり、新たに作詩されたりして、剣舞として舞われるようになります。

小説家の志賀直哉は、一九一二年（大正元年）に『呉服屋の息子で私と同年の子供が其時分流行しだした改良剣舞をやった。其後で四つ上の叔父と私と只の剣舞をした』と記しており、この頃の剣舞が、多くの人に取り組まれていたものであったことが示されています。

第二次世界大戦

日露戦争終結後の大正デモクラシー中、剣舞の人気は低迷し

sovereignty. In and after the Sino-Japanese War (1894) and the Russo-Japanese War (1904), kenbu was performed at various occasions such as army send-off parades, camp encouragement activities, and victory celebrations.

Therefore, in the early days of the Meiji period when kenbu emerged, many pieces portrayed samurai and their activities in the pre-modern age, such as "Fushikiankizan wo utsu no zu ni daisu" illustrating the fights of the military commanders of the Sengoku era, or "Shijushichishi," a piece about the forty-seven ronin and the Ako incident in the mid-Edo period. After the theory of national sovereignty had gained popularity, that was directly or indirectly addressed in many Chinese-style poems, or inspired the creation of new poems that were subsequently performed in the kenbu format.

Novelist Shiga Naoya wrote in 1912, "The textile dealer's son, who was about my own age, performed a refined form of kenbu as it was popular at the time. He later also did simple kenbu performances with me and my uncle, who was four years older." This indicates that kenbu was something that many people were involved with at the time.

World War II

Although it is said that the popularity of kenbu declined during the Taisho democracy after the end of the Russo-Japanese War, at the time of World War II, many Japanese were engaging in kenbu. Rumor has it that the founder of a certain school, who is today in his 90s and was in his teens during the war, was teaching kenbu in place of his father to soldiers who were about to depart to the battle front. My own grandmother (the first-generation head of the Seiga-ryu), who is presently 94, performed kenbu in front of army commanders as a member of an entertainment volunteer corps.

戦後

たといわれていますが、第二次世界大戦に際しては、多くの国民が剣舞に取り組みました。現在九十歳代のある流派宗家は、戦時中の十歳ほどの時に、父に代わって戦地出立前の兵士たちに剣舞を教えていたそうです。また、同じく現在九十四歳の筆者の祖母（正賀流初代宗家）は、芸能挺身隊として軍将の前で剣舞を披露しています。このように、国家の奨励のもと、女性を含む一般市民までもが町中で剣舞に取り組んだ時代でした。

敗戦後、日本を占領したGHQは、剣舞と詩吟が国民の士気高揚に酌みする芸能であるとして、剣道など他の武芸と一緒に禁令を出しました。そして解禁後は、戦前から取り組んでいた世代（筆者の祖母やそれより上の世代）とその子世代を中心に活動が再開します。「財団法人　日本吟詩舞振興会」（現・公益財団法人日本吟詩舞振興会）や、「全日本剣詩舞道連盟」といった全国組織が立ち上がり、流派を超えた活動が活発化しました。

ただ、吟剣詩舞界の中心的な担い手は、戦前の教育を受けた世代ですので、時代が変わっても、業界全体としては戦前のスタンスから大きく変化することはありませんでした。やがて高度経済成長期を迎えると、次期宗家を担う団塊世代を含め、多

From these facts we understand that it was a time when a large number of general citizens – including women – were actively engaged in kenbu in the cause of national encouragement.

After the war

After the defeat, the GHQ that occupied Japan interpreted kenbu and shigin as performing arts that aim to raise morale among the Japanese people, and eventually issued a prohibition of kenbu and other forms of martial arts such as kendo. After the ban was lifted again, it was mainly the generation that had been involved with kenbu since before the war (such as my grandmother and her seniors) and their children resumed their activities. Nationwide institutions such as the Nippon Ginkenshibu Foundation and the All Japan Kenshibudo Federation were established, and activities across different schools gained momentum.

Nonetheless, as the leading figures in the ginkenshibu scene belonged to the generation that was trained before the war, the general attitude in kenbu circles didn't change much after the war even though the times changed. The high economic growth period that followed was for a lot of people – including also the baby boomer generation that would be the next school heads to take over – synonymous with having a busy life as "corporate warriors." In the realms of culture and lifestyle, western fashion and architectural styles gained popularity, as a result of which the visibility of ginkenshibu decreased dramatically, and with it the number of people who considered taking it up as a new pastime. There are quite a few examples of kenbu schools that barely managed to save face by winning over their respective disciples' family members, relatives and acquaintances.

くの人々が企業戦士として多忙な日々を送ることになります。また生活文化面では欧米風のファッションや建築様式が流行しました。その結果、吟剣詩舞の知名度は急速に落ち、新たに始めようという人は少なくなりました。門弟の家族・親戚・知人を取り込むことで、辛うじて流派の体裁を保ってきたという流派もたくさんあります。

現代

戦後生まれの団塊世代が業界を牽引する時代になり、さらにここ十年ほどは、その子どもたちである団塊ジュニア世代が宗家を引き継ぐようになりました。流派の枠を超えて共同制作の舞台を行うなど、新しい動きが活発になりました。また、動画共有サービスやソーシャルネットワークのお陰で、以前よりも剣舞が一般の方の目に触れる機会も増えました。ゲームやアニメで侍コンテンツが脚光を浴び、それらのファンの方が剣舞を知るというケースも増えています。本書のような、一般向けの剣舞ガイド本を刊行できたことも、その象徴のように思います。

The present

Following was the era in which those born after the war and thus belonging to the baby boomer generation took the helm in the business, and in the past ten-odd years, it was the generation of their children that assumed their current positions as head of school. The new movements they initiated included collaborations in performances across the boundaries of their respective schools. Thanks to movie distribution services and social media, a lot more people than before got opportunities to encounter kenbu, and fans of games and anime naturally came across kenbu when samurai-themed contents began to attract attention. The fact that it has become possible for us to publish a kenbu guide book targeting a general readership seems to be symbolic of such recent developments.

2 これからの剣舞

芸能と時代の関係

一般的に、芸能は時の政治権力や社会情勢と深く結びついており、良くも悪くも大きく影響を受けてしまうと言われます。前項で解説したように、剣舞の歴史も、やはり明治以降の国家体制や戦争の影響を大きく受けています。特に剣舞は漢詩文という人の思想を表す「ことば」が媒介するため、特定のイデオロギーと結びつきやすい性質を持っています。また、他の芸能と比べて歴史が浅いということが、剣舞の芸能としての独立性を保つ上でウィークポイントにもなります。

例えば茶道や花道など、近代以前からの長い歴史を有するものは、戦前戦中の芸能の在り方を自省し、芸能本来の姿に立ち返りながら戦後という新しい時代を歩み始めることができました。しかしながら、剣舞は明治期に入って生まれた芸能であり、創生期の大半が戦争との関わりながらの活動であったため、戦後の平和の世においてどのような剣舞像を求めてよいか、十分

2. The Future of Kenbu

The relation between periods and performing arts

Generally, performing arts are closely related to the political and social conditions of their time, and it is commonly known that they are heavily influenced – for better or worse – by such factors. As outlined in the first paragraph above, the history of kenbu as well was greatly affected by the post-Meiji political system and the wars. As kenbu involves the medium of "verbal language" in the form of Chinese-style poetry expressing thoughts and feelings, it is by nature easy to associate with specific ideologies. In addition, its rather short history compared to other stage arts is a weak point when discussing kenbu as an independent performing art.

Practices with a long history even before the modern age, such as the tea ceremony or ikebana for example, successfully entered the new post-war era by reflecting on arts and entertainment before and during the war, and eventually returning to their original forms as performing arts. Kenbu, on the other hand, emerged as a stage art in the Meiji period, in times when performances were involuntarily affected by war matters, and it has seemingly continued to this day and age without giving proper thought to the question how to present itself fittingly in the peaceful post-war age.

Frankly speaking, considering that we are today surrounded by diverse values in daily life, we are mostly unconscious of political matters when we perform kenbu, but nonetheless, for the training and succession of the tradition of kenbu I think it is important that we brace ourselves to some extent on a regular basis. In that sense, thinking about "why to

剣舞の現代的意義

筆者は、所属する正賀流の流派活動とは別に、株式会社吟舞という会社を設立して、剣舞を広く一般の方に知ってもらおうとしています。その目的は、既に剣舞に携わっている人だけで剣舞を語るのではなく、できるだけ多くの方に触れていただくことで、多様な意見や批評に堪える芸能にしていきたいと考えているからです。ここで改めて、剣舞（吟剣詩舞）を現代人が舞うこと・観ることにどのような意味や意義があるか、筆者なりの考えをいくつか述べてみたいと思います。

な検討がなされないまま、今に至っている感があります。

現代の多様な価値観に日々触れている私達からすると、剣舞を舞う時に政治のことなどを意識することは正直ほとんど無いのですが、それでも剣舞の伝統を習い、継承していく以上は、日頃から少しは身構えておくことが必要だと考えています。そういう意味で、「なぜこの作品を選び」「どう舞うのか」について考えることは大切です。単に、「昔からある演目だから」という理由で舞い続けるだけでは、時に世間の感覚から大きくずれることがあるので注意すべきでしょう。

---

choose this particular piece" and "how to perform it" is essential. When you continue to perform a certain piece only "because it's a classic," it may happen that your performance totally misses the point in terms of sensibility, so we need to be careful in this respect.

The meaning of kenbu in the present age

In addition to my teaching activities at the Seiga-ryu that I belong to, I established the Ginbu company with the aim to widely introduce kenbu to the general public. My idea behind this was to make kenbu a performing art that stands all sorts of opinion and criticism, by involving as many different people as possible, rather than only those that have been engaged in kenbu for some time. Below I would like to share my own thoughts regarding the meaning of kenbu (ginkenshibu) performed and watched in the present age.

1. Visualizing and embodying poetry

The first point is the visual presentation of superior Chinese and Japanese waka poems through dance.

For many centuries since ancient times, the Japanese have been importing mainly Chinese culture and education based on Confucianism, such as poetry, medicine and painting, which have been incorporated in modified forms as original parts of Japanese culture. Yamato-e paintings, waka poems, and other forms of art and culture inspired by the sensitivity of the Japanese people look back on a long history as well. Many things that are today referred to as "traditionally Japanese" emerged in fact from backgrounds with both Japanese and Chinese elements. The training of kenbu can be

1. 詩歌の視覚化と体現

第一は、優れた漢詩や和歌を、演舞を通じて視覚的に見せることができる点です。

日本人は、古代から何世紀にもわたって、中国から儒学を中心に、漢詩文、漢方学、絵画など、多くの文化・教養を輸入し、日本文化の一つとして形を変えつつ受容してきました。また、大和絵や和歌など、日本人の感性から生まれた文化・芸能も長い歴史を持っています。今日「日本の伝統文化」と呼ばれるものの多くは、和と漢の両方がその背景にあります。剣舞を学ぶことは、漢詩や和歌の古典に触れ、演舞を通じてそうした先人の歩みや感性を引き継ぎ、体現できるものだといえます。

2. 日本各地の名勝や人物の魅力を発信

剣舞を通じて日本の各地域の名勝や人物を知り、地域の魅力を発信することができます。高等学校の吟剣詩舞道部が出場する全国高等学校総合文化祭では、各府県がそれぞれの地域の史跡や人物に関する漢詩や和歌を取り上げ、多くの学生が舞台芸能を通じて地域に根付く歴史や文化に触れていることがわかります。

昨今の観光ブームで、新しい観光施設を作るのも良いですが、地域本来の魅力は、その土地に暮らしたり訪れたりした多くの先人が長年語り継いできた言葉に、最も表れているよう

considered as an opportunity to come in contact with classical Chinese and Japanese poetry, pick up our forefathers' sensitivities and achievements, and embody those through our own performance.

2. Introducing scenic places and distinguished personalities of Japan

Kenbu can work as a tool for understanding and communicating the appealing regional characteristics of places across Japan, such as locations of particular scenic beauty or personalities of distinction. Participants at high school ginkenshibu club gatherings at nationwide cultural festivals often present Chinese and Japanese poems related to their respective own prefecture's historic sites and figures, which shows that performing arts are for many students a means for connecting with their own native region's historical and cultural roots. While it is surely fine to establish new facilities for the growing numbers of tourists these days, it appears to me that the original charm of each region is best communicated through the traditions handed down by our ancestors who have lived or stayed at the respective places for ages. In this sense, I consider it as a luxurious opportunity to be able to immerse myself in such verbal heritage, and communicate it through my own dance.

3. Communicating the traditional focus on the waist and belly

According to researchers in the field of somatic science, the training of kenbu is said to have a supporting effect on the indigenous physical senses of the Japanese people. Educationalist Saito Takashi points out that "the sensory center of the Japanese body used to be the waist and belly, but that seems to be getting lost." From the viewpoint of an instructor

な気がします。彼らの言葉に浸りながらそれを自身の舞で表現できるなんて、なんと贅沢な世界でしょうか。

3. 腰・ハラを中心とする身体の伝承

身体論の研究者によると、剣舞の稽古は、日本人の昔からの身体感覚を養う効果があるとされています。教育学者・斎藤孝氏は、「日本人の身体の中心感覚は『腰・ハラ』であったが、もはやそれが失われてしまっている」と指摘しています。確かに、伝統芸能の指導者の立場から見ても、例えばお祭りなどで若い男性が浴衣の帯を下腹ではなくウエスト（腰のくびれ）で締める人が多いことは気になります。西洋式の生活がすっかり定着したことで、「帯を下腹で締める」という感覚が薄れているということでしょう。

他にも、日本語の慣用句には、「腰を据える」「腰（コシ）がある」など、腰を使った表現が多いですが、もはや現代日本人はそれらの感覚を理解できない人が多いのではないでしょうか。すでに、過去の日本人と現在の日本人には身体感覚として断絶が生じているようです。

剣舞は、他の伝統芸能や武道と同様に中腰とすり足を基調とした動作が中心で、その中でも特に「腰の粘り」「ひねり」「重心の位置」などがお稽古において大事になりますから、日本人

in the realm of traditional performing arts, it is indeed a noticeable trend that, at traditional festivals for example, many young men are fastening the belts of their yukata not at the lower belly but at the waist. It seems that people have gotten so used to Western lifestyles that they have naturally lost the feeling for "fastening the belt at the lower belly." The Japanese language also has a variety of idioms that include the word "koshi" (waist), such as "koshi wo sueru (to settle down)" or "koshi ga aru (to be chewy)," whereas many young people today probably don't quite understand the sensitivity that inspired such expressions. There seems to be a break of sorts in terms of physical sensations between the Japanese people of past times and the people of today.

Like in other forms of traditional performing and martial arts, a half-sitting posture and shuffling feet are the basic body movements in kenbu as well, and as such things as "having bounce in the lower part of one's body," twist, and the center of gravity become especially important, the kenbu training is at once training and tradition of the indigenously Japanese way of using the body.

4. Succeeding to samurai culture

Finally, there is the aspect of "succession to samurai culture" that I repeatedly mention in this book. Among the Chinese and Japanese poems used in kenbu are many that were composed by samurai. The first to promote the reception of Chinese writings in Japan were Buddhist monks, but also samurai families that had been at the center of politics for a long time dedicated themselves to studies of Chinese classics and their teachings. Armed in addition with the unique psychogenic properties and philosophies of samurai, they composed Chinese-style poems in important situations in

的な身体の使い方を修練し、伝承していくことができるのです。

4・武家文化の継承

　最後に、本書でも繰り返し述べている「剣舞を通じた武家文化の継承」を挙げておきたいと思います。剣舞で扱う漢詩・和歌には、特に武士が詠んだものが多数あります。漢籍の受容にはじめに積極的に取り組んだのは仏教僧ですが、政治の中枢を長く担った武家階級も漢籍を多く学び、教養を身につけました。

　そのうえで、武士ならではの精神性や考え方を持ち、それを人生の大事な場面で漢詩として詠み、思いを残してきたのです。武士が詠んだ漢詩は、職業詩人が詠んだものと異なり、詩としては必ずしも優れたものばかりではないのですが、その分、彼らの生き様や精神、その前提にある武家社会の様子が直接的に生き生きと詠み込まれています。

　ここで、改めて「武家文化」とは何か考えてみましょう。まず「文化」の辞書的説明は「人間の知的洗練や精神的進歩とその成果」、そして「ある社会の成員が共有している行動様式や物質的側面を含めた生活様式」（ブリタニカ国際大百科事典　小項目事典）です。したがって、武家文化とは、「武士の発生から明治期の廃刀令までの七、八百年で培われた知的洗練、精神的進歩、行動様式、生活様式の総体」ということができます。

their lives in order to capture their thoughts in such particular moments. Different from those made by professional poets, Chinese-style poems made by samurai are not necessarily of superior quality as poems, but they do communicate very immediately and vividly their respective creator's lifestyle, mentality, and underlying aspects of the samurai society at large.

At this point, I would like to take a step back and examine what exactly "samurai culture" means in the first place. The definition of "culture" in dictionaries is something along the lines of "human intellectual sophistication and mental progress, and the products thereof," and "lifestyles, including behavior patterns and material aspects, that are shared by the members of a certain community." Accordingly, samurai culture can be described as "the gross of intellectual sophistication, mental progress, behavior patterns and lifestyle cultivated over the course of 700-800 years from the emergence of samurai to the ban of private possession of swords in the Meiji era."

The substance of "samurai culture" has of course changed over time, and there are large differences between the samurai of the early Sengoku era and those in the late Edo period. The term "bushido" for example, which generally expresses the lifestyle of samurai, was initially used for describing the "brave attitude of considering death on the battlefield to be the highest honor," but in addition to this notion of fighting spirit, in the early to mid-Edo period it transformed into a concept that includes also aspects of ethics in daily life in times of sustained peace. Furthermore, such samurai philosophy was not limited to the samurai class alone, but it came to represent the ethical perspective of the Japanese people in general, including also ordinary townspeople and other social classes at the time. As an example, the character of a samurai who "values faith and trust, and keeps his promise even at the hazard of his life" greatly

「武家文化」の中身は、当然ながら時代を経て変遷しており、戦国時代初期と江戸後期では大きく異なります。例えば、武士の生き方を表す「武士道」などの言葉は、初期のうちは「討ち死が最高の栄誉」といった武勇を語る時などに使われていましたが、江戸初中期からは、武士本来の戦闘者としての精神のみならず、持続的平和の時代における日常生活での倫理も含む概念になってきました。さらにこうした武士の思想は、武家階級のみに留まらず、町民など他の階級を含め、広く当時の日本人の倫理観となっていたのです。一つ例を挙げれば、武士の「信義・信用を重んじ、約諾は自己の命に替えても守りぬく」という気風は、商道徳・商行為に対しても大きく影響力を及ぼし、商売において帳簿上の差額決済をもってする信用的取引が成立する前提となっていました。こうしたことは、その後に始まる近代化の前提として大きく作用したと考えられます。

現在でも武士の思想や行動は、時代劇や映画で取り上げられたり、あるいはスポーツの日本代表団の愛称に「サムライ」が使われたりするなど、大衆の間で比較的好意的なイメージが共有されています。また、海外の人々からも日本人のイメージとして「サムライ」という言葉がよく聞かれます。武士の価値観は、現代からするともちろん相容れない点もたくさんあるのですが、これだけ世界的に「侍」が有名で注目を集めていること

affected also such things as business ethics and commercial activities, as it has become the very foundation for trustful trade and commercial transactions based on margin settlements in account books. Such things can at once be understood as having paved the way for the subsequent modernization.

The bevavior and philosophy of samurai is still being portrayed in historical plays and movies today, and also in the realm of sports, the term "samurai" often appears in the nicknames of Japanese national teams, which indicates relatively positive image it enjoys among the general public. People abroad also frequently use the term "samurai" when describing their image of the Japanese people. In contemporary contexts, many of the samurai values have of course become more or less incompatible, but it appears to me that the fact that "samurai" are so famous and regarded around the world shows that there is something in this concept that still strikes a chord with the people of today. Therefore, I believe that it is meaningful enough to use kenbu as a means for investigating into samurai culture from a contemporary point of view.

Types of poetry

For the discussion of samurai culture as illustrated in kenbu, it is extremely important to understand the circumstances under which the underlying poems were composed. Following the list of subjects of poems by era in Chapter 1, now I would like to take a closer look at the different types of poetry, divided into five categories according to their characteristics.

はやはり何かしら現代人に通じるものがあるということだと思います。剣舞を通じて、武家文化を現代人の目線で考察する意義は十分にあると思います。

詩文の類型

剣舞に表現された武家文化を考察する上で、詩歌がどのような状況で詠まれたものか理解することは非常に重要です。ここでは、詩歌の特徴を踏まえて五つに分類してみたいと思います。

① 武士が自らの人生訓や決意を詠んだもの
② 主に江戸期の武士が、自身と社会のあり方を詠んだ詩
③ 主に江戸期の武士が、過去の人物や出来事について詠んだ詩
④ 中国詩および中国文化への敬意を表す詩
⑤ 明治以後に作詩された作品

① について、
武田信玄作「偶作」（p.118）は、自らの武将としての傲りを、自らの名前を尋ねてきた僧侶によって気付かされたという内容が詠まれています。また、釈月性作「将に東遊せんとして壁に題す」は、一度故郷を離れて学びに出るからには、志を果

---

1. Poems composed by samurai as expressions of their rules and resolves in life
2. Poems composed by samurai mainly in the Edo period to illustrate their own and general social life
3. Poems composed by samurai mainly in the Edo period to extol persons or events of the past
4. Poems composed to pay tribute to Chinese poetry or Chinese culture at large
5. Poems composed in the Meiji period or later

Category 1
In his poem "Gusaku" (p.118), Takeda Shingen illustrates how a priest made him aware of his pride as a military commander when he asked his name. Shaku Gessho's "Masani toyusentoshite hekini daisu" expresses the strong determination not to return to his hometown before having achieved what he had left it for.

Category 2
Many of the poems composed by patriots in the late Tokugawa period fall into this category. The raid of the forty-seven ronin had a profound effect on society at the time as an incident that questioned the general idea of samurai, and poems themed on this subject matter belong to this category as well (p.120).

Category 3
The samurai of the Edo period captured scenes of the Genpei War and the battles of the Sengoku warlords in numerous

たすまで決して戻らないという強い決意を表しています。

②について、

幕末の志士が詠んだ詩は、多くがこの類型に分類されます。また、赤穂浪士による討ち入り事件は、武士のあり方を問う事件で、当時の社会に与えた影響は大きく、これについて詠んだ漢詩もこの類型に分類されます（P.120）。

③について、

江戸時代の武士らは、源平合戦や戦国大名の戦ぶりを多数漢詩に残しています。これは、漢詩を詠んだ作者にとって、戦国時代までの歴史が、自らの出自や精神文化に直結するルーツであることを自覚していることを物語っています。頼山陽「川中島〔不識庵機山を打つの図に題す〕」（P.34）などがこの類型に分類されます。

④について、

日本は、古来より中国から政治経済に関する制度や学問はもちろん、文学、絵画、陶芸などの多くの文化を学び、受容してきました。剣舞の舞台で、演者が紋付き袴を着用し、日本刀を用いて中国漢詩を舞うことに違和感を覚える人もいますが、過

---

poems, which shows that they had identified the immediate roots of their own descent and moral culture in the history prior to the Sengoku era of civil wars. Works in this category include also Rai Sanyou's "Kawanakajima" (p.34).

Category 4

In addition to systems and sciences related to politics and economics, Japan has been importing and adopting also many aspects of culture such as literature, painting or ceramic art from China since ancient times. It may seem odd to some that performers in kenbu pieces wear costumes combining a crested kimono and a hakama, and dance to Chinese poetry with Japanese swords, but when bearing in mind that many samurai in past times were familiar with Chinese literature, studied Chinese poetry, or even composed their own Chinese-style poems, it is not all that unnatural to express one's respect toward Chinese culture through dance.

Category 5

Works in this category include new poems, songs or ballads composed on request by modern era poets for kenbu performances or other purposes. Regarding poems written before or during the war, some works must be handled with special care.

Works that require special attention
Poems themed on emperor-centered historiography

去に多くの武士が漢籍に触れ、漢詩を学び、自らも詩作を行ったことに注目すれば、中国文化に対する敬意を持ってそれを舞うことは、そう不自然ではないと考えます。

⑤について、

近代以後の漢詩家が、剣舞や他の要望を受けて書き下ろした詩歌や、歌謡吟詠など新しい曲も含まれます。ただ、戦前戦中に作詩された作品については、取り扱いに注意を要するものもあります。

※注意したい作品

● **皇国史観を主題とした作品**

明治中期から昭和初期にかけて、剣舞が大衆に人気を博すにつれ、かつての主君への忠誠心が、国家や天皇への忠誠心に読み替えられ、天皇に忠節を尽くした人物に関する漢詩が多く制作され、演舞が行われました。その典型は、南北朝時代に後醍醐天皇に使えた楠木正成です。楠木正成は、鎌倉幕府から悪党と呼ばれますが、幕末の尊王派により忠臣として見直され、明治期に入って「大楠公」と呼ばれるようになり、修身教育でも祀られる存在となりました。しかし、戦後は価値観の転換により楠公に対しても多様な評価が行われていま

The more popularity kenbu gained among the general public from the mid-Meiji to the early Showa period, the "loyalty to one's lord" that used to be expressed in kenbu performances was replaced with "loyalty to the country and the emperor," as a result of which many poems about loyal followers of the emperor were composed and performed. A typical example is Masashige Kusunoki, who served emperor Godaigo in the Nanboku-ch period. Masashige Kusunoki had been called a villain since the Kamakura shogunate, but was reevaluated as a loyal retainer by the imperialists in the late Tokugawa period. In the Meiji period he came to be called "Dai-Nanko" and worshipped in the realm of moral training education. However the turnabout of values after the war resulted in varied evaluation of Nanko. In kenbu, works related to Nanko appear so frequently that there is at least one piece at any kenbu event today, so when performing such a piece, I think it is helpful to look at the evaluation of Kusunoki Masashige and how it changed in the course of history, and identify one's purpose as to what exactly the choreography and performance are supposed to express.

Poems based on colonialism in the modern age
One can generally say that there is no need for kenbu performers today to embrace these kinds of works. "Nireizan" by Maresuke Nogi, one of the most well-known kenbu pieces, praises the great achievements regarding the struggle for Port Arthur in the Russo-Japanese War, but when considering the situation of the people that suffered damage in the war, this is certainly one piece that performers better refrain from showing in front of non-Japanese audiences.

す。剣舞界においては、楠公作品は、発表会で必ず一度は登場するほどの頻出作品ですので、少なくとも、楠木正成の歴史的評価の変遷に目を向け、演舞する場合には何を表現する目的で振りを付け、舞うのかを明確にしておくのが良いと思います。

● **近代の植民地主義を前提とする作品**

これらは敢えて現代人が採り上げる必要性はないと考えます。

剣舞の代表作品の一つである乃木希典作「爾霊山」も、日露戦争で旅順港をめぐる日露の争奪戦での大功を詠んだもので、戦禍に見舞われた当時の人々の状況を思えば、この作品を外国の方に対して披露することは躊躇されるべきと思われます。

剣舞のオリジナリティとは

ここまで剣舞の現代的意義について考察してきましたが、改めて剣舞の芸道としてのあり方についてまとめたいと思います。

剣舞が、武士が考案した芸能であり、武道の型を昇華させて舞にした経緯を重視することは、剣舞の舞踊としてのオリジナリティになり得ると考えます。その中でも、江戸中期～後期の武士が、自分や歴史上の人物に関して、自らの考察を加えて構成

Originality in kenbu

Following my discussion of the meaning of kenbu in a contemporary context, I would like to focus once again on its artistic qualities. Kenbu is a performing art that was initially devised by samurai, and I think it is through an emphasis on the process of refining patterns from martial arts into dance that the originality of kenbu as a dance form may be defined. Let me try and think of the works that especially the samurai in the mid/late Edo period composed based on their observations regarding their own or historical figures' lives as "stereotypical kenbu pieces." The poems they wrote from their own points of view on certain events are now choreographed and performed based on interpretations from a contemporary perspective. This two-step process is something that also applies to noh and other forms of stage arts, and to me it appears to be an integral part of the very nature of performing arts in general.

The following is a possible definition that I would offer as an answer to the question, "What is kenbu?"

"Kenbu is something that illustrates the samurai culture (including martial arts, science, spirit, courtesy, customs and conduct) of the late to mid-Edo period right before the modernization of Japan, by translating it into the format of performing arts."

した詩歌を「典型的な剣舞作品」と言ってみてはどうでしょうか。ある出来事に対して、彼らの目線で作詩されたものを、現代の人が、現代人の解釈で振り付けて舞う。この二段階構造・プロセスは、能など他の舞台芸能にも当てはまることであり、伝統芸能の本質の一つでもあるような気がします。

すなわち、「剣舞とは何か」という問いに対し、「日本の近代化直前にあたる江戸中後期の武家文化〈武術、学問、精神、儀礼、習慣、所作〉を舞台芸能化し、表現するもの」という回答を提言できるのではないか、と考えています。

ディスカッション「剣舞の芸道論」

舞としての美か、侍のリアルか？

剣舞（剣詩舞）と吟で構成される吟剣詩舞道の舞台は、特に戦後、吟詠の声楽的音楽性の獲得や、日本舞踊家の詩舞への参入によって、より洗練された舞を追求し、舞台芸術としての完成度を高めてきました。昔ながらの居合的な剣舞が変わらずに演じられる一方で、年代を追うごとにバラエティに富んだ振付や技法が取り入れられ、演舞形式も従来の詩吟と邦楽器に合わせるものだけでなく、歌謡音楽や現代音楽に合わせたり、舞台照明等を駆使した演出が行われています。

こうした舞踊美学の面から舞台芸能としての剣舞を追求する取り組みは、現代人の感性や嗜好に寄り添うことで伝統的な技能を保存していく流れであり、人口の減少かつグローバル化の波をすでに迎えた日本において、必要不可欠な発想だと思いま

3. Discussion on "The Artistic Qualities of Kenbu"

Dance aesthetic or samurai reality?

Especially after the war, performers aimed to further refine the artistic qualities of ginkenshibu – a combination of kenbu (or kenshibu) and poetry recitation – by improving the musicality of poetry recitation as a form of vocal music, and involving performers of Japanese-style dance. As a result, the quality of kenbu as a form of performing arts has significantly improved, and while there are still performances in the old sword-drawing and fencing style, the variety of choreographies and techniques keeps increasing from one generation to the next. Dance styles are no longer adapted to conventional forms of recitation and Japanese traditional musical instruments, but kenbu is today also performed to folk songs or modern music, and arranged with the additional effects of stage lighting for example.

Approaches of investigating kenbu as a performing art based on such dance aesthetical aspects represent a trend toward conserving traditional skills while bowing to the contemporary taste and sensitivity, and consodering that the waves of depopulation and globalization have long arrived in Japan, I consider this concept to be absolutely essential. On the other hand, it is also true that a "lack of roughness" has been pointed out regarding expressive styles in recent years, and I do share the impression that, against the backdrop of the developments described above, recent ginkenshibu seems to be placing so much emphasis on its visual appeal as dance that the idealistic/artistic aspects are

す。

一方で、近年の表現手法が「武骨さが失われた」と指摘する人がいるのも確かです。筆者も、近年の吟剣詩舞道が、こうした取り組みの過程において、舞としての見た目の美しさを追求するあまり、却って芸道としての理念追求が手薄になってきている印象を受けることがあります。柔軟な発想で新しい表現を生み出していくと同時に、昔からある古典作品群および昔ながらの技法について、どのように引き継ぐべきか、あるいは引き継がずに変えていくべきか。言い方を変えると、剣舞の「舞踊としての美しさ」と「武士由来の無骨さ」のバランスをどう取るか、十分考慮する必要があるでしょう。

斬れる刀か、魅せる刀か

そうした視点で剣舞のあり方を考えるとき、剣詩舞家の間でよく出る議論の一つに、「その剣技では斬れない」VS「斬れるかどうかは重要ではない」というものがあります。剣舞を舞踊美学の面から追求することを強く勧め、剣詩舞界に数々の助言を行った人物に、舞踊評論家の石川健次郎氏がいます。ここでは石川氏の論説を引用しつつ、それに対する筆者の考えを述べたいと思います。

getting somewhat neglected. The task has to be to work out novel forms of artistic expression based on flexible ideas, while at once thinking about how classical pieces and techniques that have been around for a long time should be taken over - or changed without taking over original elements. In other words, the question that demands careful consideration first and foremost is how the right balance between the "beauty of dance" and the "original samurai roughness" can be achieved in kenbu.

How to kill with a sword, or how to fascinate with a sword

When discussing kenbu from such kind of perspective, one argument that often arises among kenshibu performers is rooted in such contradictive views as, "You can't kill anyone with that technique," and "It's not a matter of being able to kill someone in the first place." One man who has been strongly recommending to investigate kenbu based on dance aesthetical aspects, and who has repeatedly offered advice to kenshibu performers, is dance critic Ishikawa Kenjiro. Below is a quote from Mr. Ishikawa's theory regarding the use of swords in kenbu, followed by my own thoughts.

The movements we see in conventional kenshibu include many choreographed elements that pretend to be refining ancient swordsman skills and manners through dance, but that are in fact much more biased toward the spiritual notion of the performer's attachment to his sword than toward the artistic quality of the dance. Realistic fencing scenes as seen on TV and in movies today, or tachimawari action scenes in kabuki or historical plays, however, mostly revolve around natural postures and movements that do not display any obsessiveness with swordsman

石川氏は剣舞における剣の使い方について、下記のように述べています。

従来の剣詩舞の動きの中には、古来よりの刀法や礼法を舞踊的に磨き上げていくと云いながら、実際には舞踊性よりも刀に対する精神性に偏った振付が多く見られた。しかし現代のテレビや映画で見られる写実的な剣技の映像や、歌舞伎や時代劇の立回りは、ほとんどが自然体を主流にして、刀法や礼法と云ったこだわりを感じさせない動作が見られる。……

見習いたいのは刀剣に対するこだわりをもたずに、剣技を舞踊表現に巧みに活用している点である……剣舞の舞踊的表現とは、その刀法では〝人が斬れるか斬れないか〟が最重要課題なのではなく、舞踊的な迫力で必殺の演技を如何に見せるかというテクニックが大切だと思う。

成立当初の剣舞は、詩吟に合わせてただ居合の型を行うものでしたし、今でも、七言絶句の一句（全体の四分の一）がまるまる刀技の披露に終始することは多くみかけます。氏のいう「刀剣に対するこだわり」は、確かに多くの剣舞指導者にとって非常に強いものがあり、舞踊的な観点から剣舞を眺めた場合、表現の足かせになる可能性は確かにあります。氏としては、その

skills or manners whatsoever. What we can learn from these is how to skillfully adopt techniques of the sword in a dance performance, without excessive attachment to the sword itself. The most important thing regarding the dance element in kenbu is not the question whether or not it showcases "techniques that can kill," but in my opinion, it is the technique of convincingly showing a "killing action" through overwhelming dance moves.

At the time of its establishment, kenbu was nothing more than a succession of sword-drawing patterns performed to poetry, and even today, there are a lot of shichigon zekku (a style of Chinese poetry with seven-word lines) poems in which one phrase (one quarter of the entire poem) is dedicated to the display of swordsman skill. For many kenbu instructors, the "attachment toward the sword" as M. Ishikawa calls it is certainly a very strong factor, and when looking at kenbu from a dancing point of view, it may certainly happen that it becomes a hindrance to the artistic expressiveness. Mr. Ishikawa certainly represents the viewpoint that performers should not only exhibit such sword-drawing and fencing skills, but be more concerned about the visual beauty of their dance.

Regarding the habit of incorporating a lot of swordsman techniques into choreographies, I would consent to this to a certain degree. One reason is that kenbu was devised by samurai, and developed as a performing art that contains elements of martial arts. These elements I consider to be what defines the originality of kenbu in comparison with other performing arts. Another reason is that, as we are talking about "sword dance," there are certain expectations from the side of the spectator (or novice) – rather than the performer (or instructor) – toward the aspect of handling the sword. Especially in cases where people with experience in martial arts enter a kenbu school, or go to watch a

ように居合・抜刀術ばかり見せるのではなく、もっと舞踊として美を追求するべきだという意見があるのでしょう。

ただ、筆者はこうした刀技をたくさん振り付けに取り入れることについて、一定程度は肯定したいとも思っています。その理由の一つは、剣舞が武士によって考案され、武道要素を含みながら舞台芸能として発展してきたことが、他の芸能と異なるオリジナルの要素だと考えているからです。もう一つの理由は、「剣舞」という以上、演者（もしくは指導者）よりも、観客（もしくは入門者）が剣捌きを期待するからです。特に武道の経験がある方が剣舞教室に入門したり、舞台を鑑賞した場合、剣舞における刀剣の扱いが武道的かそうでないかに強い関心を抱く傾向があります。もし刀の扱いが武道的な観点を一切無視して、単なる舞の小道具の一つとして使われているならば、彼らにとって剣舞は非常に軟弱なものに見えることでしょう。

ある流派の家元から聞いた話ですが、「あらゆる武道を修得した者が最後に行き着くのが剣舞である」と、自らの弟子の話を聞いた経験からそう話しておられました。また私の教室にこられる生徒さんも、「剣舞の存在を知らずに殺陣を習っていたけれども、刀に対する精神性を重視する剣舞に惹かれて転向した」という方が沢山いらっしゃいます。彼らにとっては、武道的な刀技を舞の中で活用し、それによって漢詩に詠み込まれている

performance, they tend to be particularly interested to see whether the handling of the sword corresponds with martial arts techniques. If kenbu ignored the question whether or not the use of the sword complies with the rules of martial arts, and simply incorporated the sword as a gadget in the dance, it would surely become a totally spineless art from such people's point of view.

The head of a certain school once told me that "kenbu is what people skilled in various martial arts eventually all arrive at," which he had concluded from his own experience talking to his disciples. Also among the pupils at my own school, there are many who "had been studying fencing without knowing about kenbu, and then switched because of [their] admiration for kenbu as an art that values the spiritual aspect of the parformer's attitude toward the sword". For them, the ability to adopt martiual art techniques of handling a sword as parts of a dance performance, and thereby express the samurai spirit and lifestyle that the poems are all about, is at once what fuels their motivation to practice kenbu. I would go as far as to say that presenting the fighting profession itself of samurai may be considered as one valuable style of poetic expression.

Visualize spirit, or adhere to the subject matter

Another discussion revolves around the question whether the choreography of a piece should primarily focus on the subject matter (or the story or message) of a poem, or rather visualize the general underlying aspects of samurai spirit and the respective author's own lifestyle. Compared to the discussion on "techniques of handling the sword" as described in the previous paragraph, this is a somewhat abstract discourse, but like in the previous case, let me look

武士の生き様や精神を表現できることが、剣舞を修行するモチベーションにもなっているのです。戦を生業とするサムライの姿そのものを見せることも、詩心表現の一つとして考えて良いのではないでしょうか。

精神性を見せるか、主題を追うか

もう一つの議論は、振付をする時に、詩文の主題（ストーリーや主張）を追うことを重視するのか、あるいは、主題の背景となる武士の精神性や作者の生き方を重視するのか、というものです。この議論は、前項の「剣技のあり方」と比べるとやや抽象的な議論になるのですが、前項と同様、石川氏の主張を見てみましょう。

従来、剣詩舞の表現内容については、とかく観念的な精神性を尊ぶ傾向が見られた。こうした考え方を真向から否定するわけではないが、例えば剣舞に多く見られる傾向として、詩文を武士道の精神性に結びつけ、戦意高揚的な居合・抜刀術の連続動作が振付の基になって、詩の本来の意味を見失ってしまうことがある。……それらの詩文に述べられた作品の主題を掘り下げるために、とかく陥りやすい主観から一歩身を

again at Mr. Ishikawa's thoughts on this matter.

Regarding the contents of kenshibu performances, there has been a trend toward worshipping ideological spirit ("seishinsei"). While I do not flatly deny such kind of approach, as a rather prominent tendency in kenbu, there may cases in which the contents of poems are tied to the bushido spirit, and choreographies are based on a foundation of consecutive sword-drawing and sword-wielding movements aimed to increase one's fighting spirit, as a result of which the poems' original meanings get lost. In order to probe into the subject matters expressed in such poems, it is necessary to take a step back from easily assumed subjective attitudes, and interpret the respective material from an objective point of view instead, while also taking into consideration the value of performing such works as kenshibu pieces at this particular point in time, from a dance aesthetical position.

What requires attention first and foremost when discussing this matter is the difference between "spirit" and "spirituality." "Spirit" (or spiritual culture) refers to the spiritual culture that was built within the samurai society, and that contains such concepts as loyalty or sense of shame, whereas "spirituality" is a concept that focuses more on the quality of "fortitude" so to speak, as in "one can win any war as long as one possesses mental strength." A serious discussion on this topic is not possible without a clear distinction between these two.

From his text one can guess that Mr. Ishikawa is probably referring to the concept of "spiritual supremacy" when he talks about "spirit." While exclaiming that he does "not flatly deny" the habit of many kenbu performers to tie poems to

退いて、客観的に作品を読みとることと、更にその作品を現時点で剣詩舞作品として演じることの価値を舞踊美学的な立場で考えにいれたい。

この議論をする時に、はじめに注意しておくべきは、「精神性」と「精神（至上）主義」の違いです。精神性（精神文化）とは、例えば忠義の考え方や、恥に対する感覚など、武家社会において築かれてきた精神文化を指します。対して、精神（至上）主義は、例えば「己の精神力の強さがあれば必ず戦に勝つことができる」などの、いわば根性論的な考え方です。この二つを区別しないと、まともな議論にはなりません。

さて、右記の石川氏の「精神性」に関する指摘は、文面から察するに恐らく「精神至上主義」のことを指していると思われます。石川氏は、多くの剣舞家が詩文を武士道の精神性に結びつけることについて、「真向から否定するわけではない」とするものの、より舞踊美学的な立場で主題を掘り下げることを求めています。前述したとおり、剣舞は戦前に戦意高揚を目的に積極的に取り組まれていたのですが、石川氏の指摘は、戦後もその感覚が抜けないまま、精神至上主義を前面に見せるような作品がたくさんあることを示しています。そのような作品は当然ながら極めて前時代的な印象となり、舞台芸術としては、評価

the bushido spirit, Mr. Ishikawa demands at once to probe into the subject matter from a dance aesthetical position. As mentioned above, the Japanese people actively engaged in kenbu before the war with the aim to increase the soldiers' fighting spirit, but according to Mr. Ishikawa, this notion does not disappear after the war, and there are still many pieces in which the aspect of spiritual supremacy is pushed into the foreground. I think that such pieces are of course perceived as being extremely old-fashioned, and as works of performing art, they are pieces that are not given much recognition. When Mr. Ishikawa further talks about "taking a step back from easily assumed subjective attitudes," I think he wants to suggest to eliminate such subjective thinking as much as possible, and focus more on the respective poem's contents instead.

The question how to incorporate the spirit (spiritual culture) that is contained in a poem into a dance performance is in my view an indispensable consideration when it comes to choreographing a kenbu performance. Many poems that are performed as kenbu pieces were composed by samurai or priests, without necessarily pursuing the artistic quality that characterizes the works of true poets. Instead, they largely contain notions of samurai views and spirit, and in many cases that spirit itself is the central subject even more than the particular situation in which the respective poem was composed. Therefore, I think that dancing while considering the bushido spirit that every single line of the respective

されないものとなると思われます。石川氏が「とかく陥りやすい主観から一歩身を退いて」と述べているのは、振り付けをする際には、なるべくその発想を抜いて、もっと詩文の内容に向き合ってはどうかと諭しているのだと思います。

　一方で、詩に込められた精神性（精神文化）をどのように舞に織り込むか、これは剣舞を振り付ける上で不可欠な考え方だと思います。剣舞の作品として採り上げられる詩歌の多くは、武士や出家僧が詠んだものであり、必ずしも詩人としての芸術性を追求したものではありません。それだけに、武士としての人生観や精神性が多分に含まれており、その詩が詠まれた個別のシチュエーション以上に、精神性そのものが主題となっていることも多々あります。したがって、一つの詩句に対して、そこにどのような武士道の精神が詠み込まれているかを考えて舞うことは、むしろ避けるべきではないと思います。石川氏のいう「武人の心構えを象徴的に見せ、さらに舞踊美学的な立場で表現を練る」とは、そのような意図と理解して良いでしょう。

underlying poem is charged with is an approach that is not to be avoided at all. This is certainly also how Mr. Ishikawa's idea of "symbolically portraying a samurai's frame of mind, while at once refininig expressiveness from a dance aesthetical position" is to be understood.

剣舞は伝統芸能か？

トピックスの最後として、「剣舞は伝統芸能か？」という議論に触れておきたいと思います。剣舞について少し勉強された方や、他の伝統芸能に携わる方の中には、「剣舞は伝統芸能ではない」と言う方が時々いらっしゃいます。確かに、剣舞が舞台芸能として誕生したのは明治維新前後と考えるのが通例であり、芸能史としては一五〇年ほどの長さしかないので、茶華道など、室町期には形を成し始めた芸能文化の歴史からすると、比べるべくもありません。

「伝統」の辞書的な意味は、「ある民族・社会・集団の中で、思想・風俗・習慣・様式・技術・しきたりなど、規範的なものとして古くから受け継がれてきた事柄。また、それらを受け伝えること」（小学館　デジタル大辞泉）とされていますが、そもそも、「伝統」という言葉自体、明治維新後に積極的に使われるようになった言葉の一つです。つまり、茶華道などの他の芸能を含め、前近代の江戸期までに培われてきた文化・芸術が、明治維新という近代化を迎えてどのように「変わった」のか、あるいは「変わらなかったのか」「途絶えてしまったのか」「生み出されたの

Is Kenbu a Traditional Performing Art?

As a final topic, I would like to address the question whether kenbu is a form of traditional performing arts. Among those who have studied kenbu to some extent, or are engaged in other traditional performing arts, there are people who express the opinion that "kenbu is not a traditional performing art." It is common to think of kenbu as something with a history no longer than about 150 years in the realm of performing arts, as it first emerged as a stage art around the time of the Meiji restoration, so it is indeed not comparable to such forms of entertainment culture as the tea ceremony for example, which began to take shape as early as in the Muromachi period.

The Digital Daijisen (Shogakukan) defines "tradition" as a "matter of handing down or succeeding to ideas, manners and customs, styles and techniques as normative aspects in a certain ethnic group, society or community, across many generations," whereas the term "traditional" itself is one of several expressions that have come into active use only after the Meiji restoration. In other words, the core meaning of the expression "traditional" lies in the understanding how forms of art and culture that developed in the pre-modern age up to the Edo period, such as the tea ceremony, have or have not changed after the Meiji restoration and the wave of modernization it brought along; how past and present are connected, with things being either discontinued or newly created.

In the case of kenbu, we can certainly speak of something that has been "newly created" in the process of westernization. One of the motives that inspired the establishment of kenbu was to create a means for former samurai to earn a living, but at the same time it was also a tool for verifying the identity of the samurai in response to the new westernized

か」、そうした過去から現代へのつながりを把握し、どのように変容してきたかを理解することに、「伝統」という言葉の意味があるといえます。

剣舞の場合は、西洋化によって「生み出された」文化・芸術といえるでしょう。剣舞が生み出された動機の一つは元武士の生計を得る手段でしたが、同時に、欧化政策に対する武士としてのアイデンティティを確認する手段でもありました。そして、それは自然に生み出されたものではなく、廃刀令によって公に刀を持てなくなった元武士らが、逆に披露する（公演する）場を作り出すことによって、彼ら自身が近代化直前の日本人（武士）の姿を舞台芸能として残そうという考えを示した結果だといえます。そう考えると、そこには、舞台芸能としての歴史は一五〇年しかないとしても、漢詩文の教養や刀剣の使術を含め、近代以前の日本の基層文化の一つでもある、武家社会の風俗・習慣が前提になっているといえるのです。

もう一つ、芸術論・近世文化史の西山松之助は伝統の定義づけとして下記を挙げています。（一部を抜粋）
・伝統とは、新たに創出されたものが、普遍的な価値を持ち、永く後世につたわることである。
・伝統はいつもその発生原初の体験へ帰ってこれを再体験し、

policies. It did not emerge naturally, but when the former samurai were forbidden to carry a sword in public through the law banning private possession of swords, they created new occasions for presenting (performing with) their swords, surely also as an expression of their eagerness to preserve the premodern Japanese (samurai) lifestyle in the format of stage performances. But even though the resulting kenbu is only 150 years old as a performing art, it is based on the manners and customs of the samurai society as a fundamental part of Japanese culture prior to modernization, including Chinese-style poetry and swordsman skills.

Nishiyama Matsunosuke, an expert in modern cultural history, suggests the following (excerpt) as an alternative definition of "tradition."

1. Tradition is something that is newly created, and subsequently handed down across many generations with an attached universal value.
2. Tradition always involves a return to its initial experience, to be re-experienced or re-evaluated time and again.
3. Such re-experience and re-evaluation with a fresh contemporary mindset is necessary in order to hand down and preserve traditions.

Based on this interpretation, if we consider the original form of kenbu as a "stage adaptation of samurai culture," I think one may understand contemporary kenbu as a "traditional performing art" that consciously re-experiences and re-evaluates it.

或は再評価することが行われる。

・伝統が伝達され保存されるためには、新鮮な現代人の意識によって再体験・再評価されることが必要である。

ここから考えると、剣舞という芸能の本来の姿は「武家文化の舞台芸能化」であるといえます。現代人の我々がそれを自覚的に再体験・再評価することで、剣舞を「伝統芸能」と呼ぶことができるのではないかと筆者は考えています。

日本に限らず、近代化による伝統の断絶は、非西洋諸国が抱える共通の課題です。しかし、少なくとも我が国では、時代の変化に柔軟に対応しながら、創造を繰り返すことによって、多くの伝統が高度な水準で維持されてきました。もちろん、伝統だから価値がある、伝統でないものは価値がない、というようなことでは全くありませんが、日本という一つの大きな社会にとって「伝統」を残していくことは、人々の社会への信頼感、すなわち社会の連続性・恒常性を確保し、安定した社会を作っていく上で非常に大切なことだと思っています。「伝統」は、携わる人間が自覚を持つことで伝統になっていくのです。

かつて剣舞は屋外のゴザの上で舞われることも多く、剣詩舞家自身、「伝統」というイメージはほとんど持っていませんでし

Not limited to Japan alone, the discontinuation of traditions due to modernization is a problem that also other non-Western countries share. However there are – at least in this country – also numerous traditions that have been sustained on a high level through continuous creation in flexible response to the changes of the times. As a matter of course, something is not automatically valuable when it is traditional, or has no value because it has no tradition, but for the Japanese society at large I think the preservation of "traditions" is extremely important in order to maintain people's trust in society, or in other words, to ensure the continuity and constancy of society, and thereby build a stable community. "Tradition" only works as such with the consciousness of the humans it concerns.

Kenbu used to be mainly performed on mats on outdoor stages, whereas the original kenshibu performers were largely indifferent to the idea of "tradition." From around 1965, halls and stages have been built across the country, and while the number of stage performances increased little by little, so did certainly also the public awareness of kenbu as a performing art. Even Chinese-style poetry, which has become rather difficult to understand for people in general today, must have felt "classically Japanese" enough to performers and spectators alike when recited with unique melodies, and danced to dressed in kimono and hakama.

When thinking about it this way, while not forgetting that "war propaganda" notion of kenbu that the "poetry=ideology" and "sword=weapon" allegories evoke, the eagerness to project a modern image of "samurai" that are well-known and highly evaluated around the world is certainly strong enough to ensure that kenbu remains as a traditional performing art for the next 100 years. Kenbu teaches us about the various forms of culture that the samurai have cultivated over

た。昭和四十年頃から、各地でホールや舞台が作られ、少しず
つ舞台で披露する機会が増えるにつれ、舞台芸能としての自覚
を高めるようになったと思われます。そして現代では、一般の
人がもはや理解しにくくなった漢詩文を、独特の節調で吟じ、そ
れを着物と袴を着用して舞うことは、演じる側にとっても、鑑
賞する側にとっても、十分に古典的で日本的なものに映るので
はないかと思います。

そう考えると、剣舞が、「漢詩＝思想」と「刀＝武器」という
戦意高揚と結びつきやすい性質があることに注意を払いつつ、世
界でも高い認知度と評価を受ける「武士」の、現代に通じる姿
を演じようとすることで、これから一〇〇年後も、伝統芸能と
して残っていくことが期待できるのではないでしょうか。剣舞
に接することで、私達は、武士が何世紀にもわたって培ったあ
らゆる文化を学び、「時代の連続性」を感じるとともに、それら
を現代人の目線で考察することができるのです。

コラム：家元制度と型

日本人の私たちにとって、数ある伝統文化・芸能が
家元制度によって成り立っていることは、漠然となが
らも当然のことと受けとめられていることでしょう。一

the course of several centuries, and enables us to observe that culture and its "continuity across the ages" from a contemporary point of view.

方、海外の方にとってはイマイチ感覚的に理解がしづらいようです。

そもそも芸能は、数値化して評価することが不可能な分野であり、それを体系的に指導するには何らかの「美の基準」が必要となります。日本の芸道の場合、それを「型」に求めた、ということができるでしょう。芸道継承の手段を家元制に求める場合、「型」の存在が流儀を定めることになります。どの流派にも共通する型も多くありますが、流派固有の「型」となると、何世代にもまたがって繰り返すうちに独特の技として磨かれており、他の流派の者が見よう見まねでやってみたところで、完全な美を描くことは困難です。

日本の芸能においては、型をそのまま真似ることが重視され、それが達成されてから先の段階に移るべきと強調されます。それは、型がすでに完成された「美」となるほどに洗練を重ねたものであることの現れと考えるからです。日本の多くの伝統工芸や芸能が、今に至るまで高い水準で保存され、海外から評価を受けるのは、ここで述べた師匠・弟子間における「完全一致」を目指す考え方があったからに他なりません。

The iemoto system and kata

For us Japanese, the fact that various forms of traditional culture and performing arts have been established based on the iemoto system is something that we certainly grasp – if only vaguely – as a matter of course, while for people overseas it seems to be a bit difficult to understand on an instinctive level.

In the realm of performing arts, it is impossible to express the value of a work through numbers, which is why systematic training needs to be based on some kind of "aesthetic standard." In the case of Japanese traditional arts, one can say that such aesthetic standard has been pursued in the form of kata (patterns). Where the tradition of such arts is subject to the iemoto system, the kata are what defines the respective school's style. While there exist many kata that are shared by all schools, there are others that are unique to each school, and that are continuously refined as original skills in the course of tradition across several generations. For members of other schools, it is difficult to reproduce these with perfect beauty through learning by watching alone.

In Japanese performing arts, special value is attached to the formal imitation of kata, with an emphasis on the idea that this has to be accomplished first before proceeding to the next level. This is because kata are being considered as manifestations of "perfect beauty" resulting from a process of repeated sophistication. Many traditional Japanese arts and crafts have been preserved to this day at a high standard, and it is surely thanks to the mindset striving for a "perfect harmony" between the master and his disciples as described above, that they have been receive such high commendation from abroad.

全国の宗家に
インタビュー

Interviews with
the Heads of
Kenbu Schools
Across Japan

大日本正義流四代宗家

多田正晃先生

▼流派の成り立ちは？

明治十九年に新潟の僧家に生まれた多田正義は、明治三十八年に神刀流の木崎正道先生に入門したのち、指導者として独立して明治四十三年に創流しました。親と道場を十軒開く約束を交わし、寺を継ぐことなく剣舞に注力したそうです。昭和二年に大阪に移住し、流派本部としました。昭和五十三年に後継者として多田正満が三代目宗家に（現・宗主）、平成十九年にその息子である私が四代目を継承しました。

▼宗家自身と剣舞との関わりは？

幼い頃から稽古を始め、三歳で初舞台を踏みました。その後、

Interview 1

Tada Masateru
Fourth-generation head of the Dai Nippon Seigi-ryu

Please tell us about the history of your school.

Tada Masayoshi, who was born the son of a Buddhist priest in 1886 in Niigata, entered Kisaki Masamichi's Shinto-ryu in 1905, and eventually founded the school in 1910 as an independent instructor. It is said that he promised his parents to open a total of ten dojo training halls, and went on to focus on kenbu instead of taking over the temple. He relocated to Osaka in 1927, where he set up the school's headquarters. In 1978, my father (and present head) Tada Masamitsu took over as third-generation head, followed by myself as the fourth generation in 2007.

How about your own involvment with kenbu?

I started practicing when I was a little kid, and I stood on a stage for the first time when I was three. After that, as a junior

中学・高校では稽古にも舞台にも出ずサッカーや柔道に明け暮れましたが、親から剣舞をしろと厳しく言われたことはありませんでした。後を継ぐのは大変なことだと分かっていたからだと思います。十八歳の時に舞台の人手が足りず、頼まれて出演したことをきっかけに、再び剣舞を始めたんです。父のお弟子さんに教えてもらいながら修行を続け、平成十四年、二十八歳

道場の様子

high and high school student, I would spend my time playing football or doing judo rather than practicing, and my parents never strictly told me to do kenbu. I think that's because they were aware of the fact that taking over the school was a difficult thing. When I was asked to fill in because there were performers missing when I was 18, that was the occasion that brought me back to kenbu. I trained under my father's pupil, and in 2002, at the age of 28, I managed to

の時に全国コンクールで優勝することができました。平成九年の創流九十周年記念大会で四代目宗家継承予定者として発表され、十年後の百周年記念大会で宗家を継承しました。周りの期待を感じ、力が入ります。

▼近年の剣詩舞界をどう感じますか？

各流派の距離が近くなったのは大きな変化でしょう。宗家の親同士の仲が良いのが大きな理由だと思います。

▼好きな作品は？

初代宗家が作った昔の剣舞です。「残月（暁に発す）」、「児島高徳」、「棄児行」などですが、実際には、演目の長さの問題や、今の詩吟音楽とは合わせにくいため、なかなか人前で演奏する機会はありません。それと「殺陣本能寺」。木刀で四人が主人公に切りかかるのですが、五十年前から同じ振り付けなんです。

▼どんな舞台で演じているのですか？

清和源氏の発祥といわれている多田神社で毎年奉納演舞をしています。国立文楽劇場では二年に一回、橿原神宮では毎年二月十一日に舞台があります。その他は名流大会や武道館大会などです。

win a national competition. At an event celebrating the 90th anniversary of the school's foundation in 1997, I was announced as successor, and eventually took over as fourth-generation head at the occasion of the 100th anniversary ten years later. I'm doing my best to fulfill the expectations that I'm sensing from the people around me.

What is your impression of the kenbu scene in recent years?

One thing that has changed significantly is certainly that the differences between the individual schools have become smaller, which mainly seems to be related to the fact that the heads are all getting along well with each other.

What are your favorite pieces?

The old kenbu pieces by the first-generation head, such as "Zangetsu (Akatsuki ni hassu),""Kojima Takanori" and "Kijiko." But as they are either too long or difficult to combine with current recitation music, I rarely get to perform them in front of people. I also like "Tate Honnoji." It's a story about four people being stabbed by the protagonist with a wooden sword, and the choreography hasn't changed in fifty years.

What kinds of performances are you doing?

We do annual dedication performances at the Tada Shrine, the alleged birth-place of the Seiwa Genji clan. There are biennial performances at the National Bunraku Theatre, and every year on February 11th at Kashihara Jingu. Besides these, we participate in the annual events with performers from the leading schools across Japan, and in shows at the Budokan.

▼どこで習えるのですか?

大阪の本部道場の他、北から北海道、名古屋、岐阜、京都、奈良、和歌山、福岡、長崎、大分に教室があります。

▼流派の特徴は?

昔ながらの踏み足を大事にしています。特に後ろ重心のまま足を出すのは他の流派ではあまり見ない所作でしょう。また、手足を大きく動かして全身を幅広く使う動きが多いのも特徴です。これは、戦後ラジオ体操が普及した時に、剣舞もそのイメージを取り入れて普及させようとしたという背景があります。

▼最後に、これからの剣詩舞界に思うことを教えてください。

剣舞は一般に思われているほど敷居が高いものではありません。賛否はあるかもしれませんが、SNSやYoutubeなども活用してもっと普及させていきたいです。そのうち、ビデオ通話やVRを使った遠隔指導が始まるかもしれません。

Where do you teach kenbu?

In addition to the main dojo in Osaka, there are branches in Hokkaido, Nagoya, Gifu, Kyoto, Nara, Wakayama, Fukuoka, Nagasaki and Oita.

What is the most characteritic feature of your school?

The school has always placed importance on the steps. Especially the posture of putting out one's leg while keeping the weight on the other leg is something that not many other schools do. Another characteristic is that we incorporate a lot of big and sweeping movements of arms and legs, and using the entire body. This partly originates from attempts to popularize kenbu by incorporating the image of "radio gymnastics" that had become popular after the war.

Finally, what are your ideas regarding kenbu in the future?

Kenbu is not as difficult to approach as people generally think. There may be pros and cons, but generally I'd like to use also such things as social media or Youtube in order to introduce kenbu to a broader audience. Maybe there will be forms of remote instruction utilizing video conference or VR technologies in the future.

小天真道流六世宗家
石田翔祥 先生

▼流派の成り立ちは？

始祖は肥後細川候の武道指南役であった福島多十朗真道（文政五年―明治二三年）。五歳年下の西郷隆盛と親交が深かった。当初から今でいう剣舞をしていたかどうかは不明で、おそらく二世宗家から撃剣興行に携わり、三世宗家・福島小天先生から近代剣舞をするようになったのだと思われます。三世宗家から流派本部が大分に移りました。それまでは世襲でしたが、私が直接師事した四世宗家・工藤天祥先生より、世襲ではなくなりました。

Interview 2

Ishida Shosho
Sixth-generation head of the Shoten Shindo-ryu

Please tell us about the history of your school.

The school was founded by Fukushima Tajuro Masamichi (1822-1890), a fencing instructor from the Hosokawa clan in Kumamoto. He was five years older than Saigo Takamori, with whom he maintained a close friendship. It is unclear whether the school was involved from the beginning in what is today known as kenbu, but it is said that the second-generation head was engaged in fencing performances, and the school started focusing on modern kenbu from the time of the third head, Fukushima Shoten.

That was also when the school's headquarters relocated to Oita. Up to that point, the school had adopted the hereditary system, but that changed with the fourth-generation head, my own teacher Kudo Tensho.

What brought you to kenbu?

I started with shigin when I was in my twenties. At the age of 28, at a shigin event, I was invited by the fourth-generation

▼ 剣舞を始めたきっかけは？

二十代から淡窓伝光霊流で詩吟を習いはじめました。二十八歳の時、詩吟の大会で四世宗家に誘われ、次の週から入門しました。以来、「今やれることは全力でやる」という思いで稽古を続けてきました。はじめは公民館などを借りていましたが、早朝は貸してもらえないので、近くの神社にお願いし、神楽殿をお借りして朝夕毎日稽古が出来るようになりました。そのうち、息子も一生懸命やってくれるようになったので、思い切って今の住所に自宅と道場を建てました。

五世宗家から次の宗家を継いでほしいと言われた時には相当悩みました。自分で一派を興すのは簡単ですが、何代も続いた流派を継ぐのには重責が伴います。今は五世から継承したものを七世にバトンタッチする役割を全うしようという気持ちでやっています。

大分市芸能まわり舞台（2020年）

head of the school, and joined the school right in the following week. From that point on, I continued my training based on the idea to "do what I can, and with every effort." I started with sessions at a public hall, but they wouldn't let me use the space early in the morning. As I wanted to train from morning to night, I eventually pleaded to a nearby shrine to let me use their kagura hall, and there I finally got to train all day long. When my son joined me quite enthusiastically somewhere along the way, I decided to build a new house with a training dojo at the current address.

When I was asked to take over from the fifth head of the school, I had a really hard time making my mind up. To establish one's own school is easy, but a school that has been around for generations is quite a heavy burden to take over. Right now I'm operating with the idea in mind to pass the things I have inherited from the fifth-generation head on to the next, the seventh head.

▼どんな舞台で演じているのですか？

全国の神社の総本山である宇佐神宮や護国神社の春季・秋季例大祭での奉納演舞をしています。また、刑務所や老人ホーム、敬老会などの慰問活動にも力を入れています。

▼どこで剣舞を習えますか？

自宅道場のほか、大分市内、宇佐高田市、国東市、杵築市に教場があり、三歳から九十歳までの方が楽しんでいます。

▼好きな作品は？

「巌流島」「坂本龍馬」「四十七士」などですね。大河ドラマなどでもよく知られている題材は、必ずしも史実どおりではなく、ドラマチックに脚色されていますが、剣舞も同様に剣舞を初めて観る方にも分かりやすく興味を持っても

稽古風景

What kinds of performances are you doing?

Next to events hosted by the kenbu and shigin organizations that I belong to, there are events held in connection with shrines and Buddhist temples, including performances at the Usajingu Shrine, the main Shinto shrine in Japan, and dedication dance at annual spring and autumn festivals at such places as the Gokoku Shrine in Oita Prefecture. As I dance in front of the gods, I'm of course wearing new tabi, but these performances take place on stone pavement, so the socks are usually ragged after a single performance.

I'm also engaging in consolation activities at prisons and homes for elderly people among others.

Where do you teach kenbu?

In addition to the training dojo at my own house in Oita, there are places in Usatakada, Kunisaki and Kitsuki. The ages of my current students range from 4 up to 96.

What are your favorite pieces?

That would be "Ganryujima," "Sakamoto Ryoma" and "Shijushichishi." Stories that are well known from such TV programs as the NHK Taiga drama series are usually dramatized and don't necessarily adhere to historical facts, and I think that such kind of choreography is also necessary in kenbu in order to arouse people's interest, or to make the subject matter easier to understand for those who watch a performance for the first time.

らえるような振り付けが必要だと考えています。

▼ 流派の特徴は?

剣舞である以上、居合道を基礎とした刃筋や刀法にこだわりがあります。舞の部分は舞として、刀を抜き始めたら武人であるべきで、刃筋を立てて演舞することだと考えています。

▼ 良い舞手になるためのアドバイスをお願いします。

とにかく研究と稽古あるのみですが、指導者は同じなのに他の生徒よりも上達の早い人は、指導者の話しを良く聞き、良く質問をする。習い方が上手な人だと思います。教え方も大事ですが、受け取り方のほうがより大事です。

▼ 最後に、最近の取り組みを教えてください。

少子高齢化と趣味の多様化で、吟剣詩舞道に携わる人達の減少に歯止めがかかりませんので、保育園や小・中・高等学校へ指導に行くなど、幼少年の育成に努めています。また、中国の子供達への指導や他の芸能団体とコラボする舞台を作っています。

What is the most characteritic feature of your school?

As kenbu is dance with a sword, we place great importance on such things as techniques and patterns of brandishing the sword. Dance is dance, but in my view the performer should behave as a warrior from the moment he begins to unsheathe the sword. When you're familiar with techiques of handling the sword, you understand from the side - right or left - on which the performer puts his sword on the floor whether he is facing a friend or an enemy. The handling of the sword is also elemental for doing postures.

What would you advise students to do to become a good performer?

It's all about studying and practicing. Those who become better than the others even though they practice under the same coach are just particularly good at learning things. One advice would be to keep asking questions, so that the coach knows at any given point where you stand and if you could follow him. How to teach things is important, but I think it's even more important how you receive and work with them.

Finally, please tell us about your most recent projects.

I'm recently putting effort especially in the training of children, to prevent ginken shimai from dying out. I'm teaching at elementary, junior high and high schools, and I established a special training club at the elementary school.

日本壮心流宗家三世
入倉昭山先生

▼ 流派の成り立ちは？

流祖・初代入倉昭星は山梨生まれ。明治三十八年、たまたま横須賀に赴いた時に大道芸で剣舞を観て、「これぞ我が道なり」と運命を感じたそうです。それから独学で剣舞を研究し、大正三年に豊橋を安住の地と定めたと聞いています。二代目は剣舞に加え、居合と詩舞を取り入れました。当時、弟子は三十人ほどでしたが、そこから少しずつ教室を広げ、一時は二千人ほどにもなりました。現在は、愛知・静岡・岐阜を中心に、東京や九州にも支部があります。

Interview 4

Irikura Shozan
Third-generation head of
the Nippon Soshin-ryu

Please tell us about the history of your school.

The founder and first-generation head, Irikura Shosei was born in Yamanashi. It is said that he happened to see a kenbu stereet performance in Yokosuka in 1905, and felt that this was the path he "was destined to pursue." He started studying kenbu by himself, and in 1914 he settled down in Toyohashi. The second-generation head introduced next to kenbu also iaido and shimai. At the time the school had about 30 pupils, and from there it gradually expanded, up to a point when the number temporarily exceeded 2,000. The school is presently based mainly in Aichi, Shizuoka and Gifu, but there are branches also in Tokyo and Kyushu.

▼ 宗家自身と剣舞との関わりは?

二代目の長男として生まれたときから跡取りとして育てられ、二歳から稽古を始めました。

▼ どんな舞台で演じているのですか?

湊神明社に流統碑と舞扇碑という流派ゆかりの碑が建っており、そこで毎年元旦に剣舞・詩舞・居合の初斬りを披露します。また四月には、舞扇供養祭を行っています。また、年一度、日本武道館で開催される全国吟剣詩舞道大会も大切にしています。故・笹川鎮江先生の吟による「兜」を三十人くらいの群舞で演じたこともあります。

稽古風景

How did you get involved with kenbu?

I was born the eldest son of the school's second-generation head, so I've been raised as his successor from the beginning. I started practicing when I was two years old.

What kinds of performances are you doing?

There is a monument commemorating the schools foundation, together with a stone monument of a fan, at the Minato Shinmeisha shrine, and every year on New year's Day we do kenbu, shimai and iaido performances there. There is also an annual fan dance festival in April. Another occasion that is very important to us is the annual big ginkenshibu festival at the Nippon Budokan. We once did a group dance with about 30 performers to the late great Sasakawa Shizue's recitation of "Kabuto" at that occasion.

▼ 好きな作品は?

大鳥圭介「五稜郭の戦い」です。刺子の道着に素足という素朴な衣装で、振り付けは五十年も前のものですが、これこそが私の剣舞の原点だと感じています。

▼ 流派の特徴は?

「板割り剣武」と呼んでいます。字の通り、お稽古場の床を足で破ってしまうほどに、強く踏み出しを行うことが特徴です。

▼ 最後に、最近の取り組みや、今後の目標を教えてください。

一般の人に広く剣舞を知ってもらうことが目標です。そのために、人気バンドやアニメ作品など、多彩な芸能・メディアとのコラボレーションを積極的に行っています。

湊神明社の流統碑と舞扇碑

What are your favorite pieces?

My favorite is Otori Keisuke's "Goryokaku no tatakai." The choreography is 50 years old, and the piece is performed in a simple quilted suit and with bare feet, but this is exactly where I'm sensing the roots of my own kenbu.

What is the most characteritic feature of your school?

The most characteristic style of our school is what we call "itawari kenbu," referring to dance steps that are so hard and strong that they almost split the stage's floorboards.

Finally, please tell us about your most recent projects.

The goal is to make kenbu widely known among the general public. In order to achieve this, we have been actively collaborating with people from a variety of genres and media, including popular music and anime among others.

人気ロックバンド「和楽器バンド」とのコラボレーション

京都本社の受付

気軽に
剣舞の世界に触れられる！

サムライ剣舞シアター（京都・東京）

二〇一四年に京都・東山にオープンした「サムライ剣舞シアター」は、本書の著者でもある鈎逢賀（正賀流継承者）が、「剣舞の間口を広げる」ことをコンセプトに設立した演舞場兼道場です。

剣舞を観たことがない人向けに構成された約一時間のステージ公演や、実際に刀を持って剣舞のお稽古を体験する「レッスン」を開催しています。剣舞や武士文化に興味のある人が気軽に訪れることができます。二〇一七年には東京・新富町に東京支店もオープンしました。

観光口コミサイト「トリップアドバイザー」で五年連続でエクセレンス認定を獲得し、毎年国内外から五千名を超える人々が訪れています。

Samurai Kenbu Theater
(Kyoto, Tokyo)
- A casual kenbu experience

The "Samurai Kenbu Theater" is a training and performance hall in Higashiyama, Kyoto. It was established in 2014 by Magari Auga (successor of the Seiga-ryu and the author of this book) with the general aim to "increase the presence of kenbu." Programs offered here include performances of about one hour, designed especially for people who have never seen kenbu before, as well as trial lessons where participants can try and practice kenbu with actual swords. The place welcomes any visitor with an interest in kenbu and samurai culture. Samurai Kenbu Theater received a Certificate of Excellence on the travel platform TripAdvisor for five years in a row, and is visited by more than 5,000 travelers from Japan and abroad every year. Tokyo Samurai Kenbu opened in 2017 in Shintomicho, Tokyo.

著者（中央）と京都スタッフ

プログラム　**Program**

デモンストレーション・ショー
（剣舞鑑賞）

剣舞師範3〜4名による、1時間の剣舞ステージ。簡単な説明のあと、古典的な剣舞、詩舞が披露されます。また、武士の文化や習慣について、実演を交えながら紹介があり、「侍と忍者の違い」や、「武家の女性について」など、外国の方が特に疑問に思うテーマも解説をしています。ステージ後半は、現代音楽を使用した創作作品。歴史物語をベースに、演者たちがドラマティックに演じます。

〈京都のみ〉
開催日時　月・火・木・土　17:15〜
（詳細はウェブサイトで確認のこと）
料金：大人3000円／子ども（5〜11歳）2000円
（税込　・2020年1月現在）

Demonstration (kenbu show)

This is a one-hour performance by a total of three or four kenbu instructors. Following a brief introduction to the basics of kenbu, they first show a classical kenbu piece with shigin recitation of Chinese-style poetry, and after that, a piece performed with a fan only (a so-called shimai or ogimai variant of kenbu) to a Japanese waka poem. The performances are interspersed with explanations about the culture and customs of samurai, including such topics as "the difference between samurai and ninja" and "the role of women in samurai families" that especially foreign visitors tend to be concerned about. The piece shown in the second half is a dramatic rendition of historical material, performed to contemporary music.

Kyoto dojo

Hours: Mon, Tue, Thu, Sat 17:15- (please visit the website for more details)
Admission: Adults 3,000 yen (tax included), children (aged 5-11) 2,000 yen (tax included)
(as of January 2020)

サムライ剣舞　体験レッスン

教室で行われているお稽古を一回完結型にした体験レッスンです。着物と袴を身に着け、座礼、刀の扱い方、扇の扱い方、すり足などのお稽古をします。講師のアドバイスでポーズ写真をいくつか撮ったら、お稽古のまとめとして、習ったことを組み合わせて漢詩の一節を詩吟に合わせて振付を舞います。本格的な伝統文化体験・サムライ体験は、旅の思い出として長く記憶に残ることでしょう。

〈京都・東京共通〉

料金：60分コース　7000円／90分コース　9000円
　　　子ども（5〜11歳）は1000円引
（税込・2020年1月現在）
開催日時はウェブサイトで確認のこと。

Samurai Kenbu trial lesson

Also offered are one-off comprehensive trial lessons that allow visitors to participate in the school's kenbu practice. Dressed in kimono and hakama, participants learn how to bow while seated, handle a sword and a fan, and do the shuffling walk. Following the instructors' advice regarding gestures, they pose for a set of souvenir photos, before the practice is wrapped up with a short performance of the practiced movements choreographed to a poem. The lesson will surely create a lasting memory of every visitor's in-depth experience of traditional and samurai culture during their stay.

Kyoto and Tokyo dojo

Admission: 60-minute course 7,000 yen (tax included), 90-minute course 9,000 yen (tax included), 1,000 yen discount for children (aged 5-11)
(as of January 2020)
For information on days and times please visit the website.

Data

（2020年2月現在）

Information (as of February 2019)

Samurai Kenbu Theater (Kyoto dojo)
35-7 Sanchome, Higashiyama-ku, Kyoto, Japan
605-0005
Gozan Hotel B1F
075-751-2033

Tokyo Samurai Kenbu (Tokyo dojo)
1-19-7 Shintomi, Chuo-ku, Tokyo, Japan
104-0041
Akuta Awazu Bldg. 5F
03-6882-5609

info@samurai-kenbu.jp
www.samurai-kenbu.jp

〈京都本社〉サムライ剣舞シアター

住所 京都市東山区三町目35-7
　　　三条花見東入ル　GOZAN地下1階
電話 075-751-2033

〈東京支店〉東京サムライ剣舞

住所 東京都中央区 新富1-19-7
　　　アクタアワーズ京橋ビル 5F
電話 03-6882-5609

運営　株式会社吟舞
info@samurai-kenbu.jp
www.samurai-kenbu.jp

●本書で紹介した教室連絡先

大日本正義流剣舞術

本部所在地	大阪市旭区森小路2-10-3
代表者	四代目宗家　多田正晃
主な教場	大阪府・京都府・福岡県・長崎県
連絡先	06-6951-6264

小天真道流剣舞道

本部所在地	大分県大分市葛木115-32
代表者	六世宗家　石田翔祥
主な教場	大分県・京都府
連絡先	097-527-7030

http://oita-kenbu.blog.jp

日本壮心流

本部所在地	愛知県豊橋市西岩田5-8-5
代表者	宗家三世　入倉昭山
主な教場	愛知県・東京都・静岡県・岐阜県・茨城県・千葉県・福岡県
連絡先	0532-63-3651

https://kenshibudo.amebaownd.com

正賀流吟舞社

本部所在地	滋賀県大津市朝日が丘1-4-6
代表者	宗家　鈎正滋、宗家二代目　鈎正賀
主な教場	滋賀県・京都府・埼玉県・東京都・岐阜県
連絡先	077-522-5621

●著者の開催教室

● サムライ剣舞シアター　教室部門
● 東京サムライ剣舞　教室部門
　　（連絡先は右頁参照）

上記の他にも全国の剣舞教室をご紹介いたします。
お気軽にお問い合わせください。

著者紹介
Author

鉤　逢賀 （まがり・おうが）
株式会社吟舞　代表取締役

滋賀県高島市出身。「文化の日」生まれ。幼少より正賀
流宗家である祖母の鉤正滋、および父の鉤正賀から剣舞
の手ほどきを受ける。滋賀大学経済学部卒業後、日本電
産（株）勤務を経て、2010年より流派活動に専念。2014
年に京都市にてサムライ剣舞株式会社（現・株式会社吟
舞）を設立、「サムライ剣舞シアター」（京都市東山区）と
「東京サムライ剣舞」（東京都中央区）の二拠点で、流派
を超えた剣舞の普及活動とプロ人材育成を始める。2017
年に京都造形芸術大学通信教育部「和の伝統文化コー
ス」を卒業。2020年秋公開予定の映画「戦国ガールと剣
道ボーイ」に出演予定。京都市在住。

Magari Auga
Representative director of Gimbu Co., Ltd.

Born in Takashima, Shiga, on the day that is celebrated as "Culture Day"
in Japan. She was introduced to kenbu at a young age by her
grandmother and originator of the Seiga-ryu kenbu school, Magari
Seishi, and by her father, Magari Seiga. Graduated from Shiga
Universi-ty's Faculty of Economics, and worked for Nidec Corporation,
before devoting herself to school activities since 2010. Established
Samurai Kenbu Co., Ltd. (now Gimbu Co., Ltd.) in Kyoto in 2014, and
began to engage in the promotion of kenbu also outside the school,
and in the training of specialized per-sonnel. Graduated from the
Japanese Traditional Culture Course at the Dis-tance Learning
Department of the Kyoto University of Art and Design in 2017, and
will appear in the movie "Sengoku Girl & Kendo Boy," to be released in
the fall of 2020. She currently lives in Kyoto.

【撮影】
吉田亮人　P2-7, 37, 38, 46, 47, 93, 109, 174-176, 178
村西一海（公益財団法人日本吟剣詩舞振興会）P27, 48, 71, 107, 171, 173, 177

【写真協力】
石田飛祥　（株式会社吟舞、小天真道流）
木村映貴　（株式会社吟舞、北辰神桜流）
鉤隆之介　（株式会社吟舞、正賀流）
鞆田邦賀　（株式会社吟舞、正賀流）
柚木京加　（株式会社吟舞、正賀流）

松葉実水　（詩道楠水吟詠会）
吾妻徳穂　（日本舞踊）
花柳寿楽　（日本舞踊）
小天真道流剣舞道の皆さん

【写真提供】
公益財団法人日本吟剣詩舞振興会
公益社団法人日本舞踊協会

【参考文献】
公益財団法人日本吟剣詩舞振興会広報誌 『吟と舞』
高橋昌明『武士の日本史』（岩波新書、2018年）
笠谷和比古『武士道の精神史』（ちくま新書、2017年）
笠谷和比古『武士道－侍社会の文化と倫理』（NTT出版、2014年）
野村朋弘『日本文化の源流を探る伝統を読みなおす1』（幻冬舎、2014年）
樫村愛子『ネオリベラリズムの精神分析－なぜ伝統や文化が求められるのか』（光文社新書、2007年）
形の文化会編『形の文化誌［9］』「芸道の形」（工作舎、2002年）
斎藤孝『身体感覚を取り戻す腰・ハラ文化の再生』（NTT出版、2000年）
剣道日本編集部編『新版　全日本剣道連盟居合』（スキージャーナル、1990年）
大野正一『剣舞の歴史』（1976年）
志賀直哉『母の死と新しい母』（1912年）

【参考webサイト】
公益財団法人 日本吟剣詩舞振興会　http://www.ginken.or.jp
公益社団法人 関西吟詩文化協会　http://www.kangin.or.jp
バーチャル刀剣博物館　https://www.touken-world.jp

【図版クレジット】
国立博物館所蔵品統合検索システム　P50, 54

Special thanks to
Yamamoto Hiroki, Bilal Chamsine